Should I HOME SCHOOL?

How to Decide What's Right for You & Your Child

ELIZABETH & DAN HAMILTON

InterVarsity Press
Downers Grove, Illinois

InterVarsity Press® is the book-publishing division of InterVarsity Christian Fellowship®, a student movement active on campus at hundreds of universities, colleges and schools of nursing in the United States of America, and a member movement of the International Fellowship of Evangelical Students. For information about local and regional activities, write Public Relations Dept., InterVarsity Christian Fellowship, 6400 Schroeder Rd., P.O. Box 7895, Madison, WI 53707-7895.

Cover illustration: Roberta Polfus

ISBN 0-8308-1976-2

Printed in the United States of America ♾

Library of Congress Cataloging-in-Publication Data

Hamilton, Elizabeth Guignard.
   Should I home school? : how to decide what's right for you & your child / Elizabeth and Dan Hamilton.
     p. cm.
   Includes bibliographical references (p.).
   ISBN 0-8308-1976-2 (alk. paper)
     1. Home schooling—United States.   I. Hamilton, Dan. II. Title.
LC40.H36   1997
371.04'2—dc21   97-19046
                                                        CIP

| 20 | 19 | 18 | 17 | 16 | 15 | 14 | 13 | 12 | 11 | 10 | 9 | 8 | 7 | 6 | 5 | 4 | 3 | 2 | 1 |

| 14 | 13 | 12 | 11 | 10 | 09 | 08 | 07 | 06 | 05 | 04 | 03 | 02 | 01 | 00 | 99 | 98 | 97 |

For parents who watch where they step
so their little ones can follow them safely Home.
Watch the path of your feet,
and all your ways will be established.
Proverbs 4:26 NASB
A righteous man who walks in his integrity—
how blessed are his sons after him.
Proverbs 20:7 NASB

Acknowledgments

Thanks to all the individuals who so willingly answered our questions and filled out our questionnaires. Your loving support made this book a reality.

An extra special thank-you to Jennifer and Andrew for giving us the material to share and the love to enjoy for now and forever.

1
Why Are You Reading This Book?

You probably have children.

You need to educate them . . . somehow.

Perhaps you are disappointed with the public school system. Or perhaps you have friends or family who have made you aware of the home-schooling option.

You have heard the claims made by both sides of the debate, and you wonder just where the hidden bias lurks in the stories and the statistics.

The issue comes down to the question, Is home schooling right for *you* and *your* family?

The answer is . . . maybe.

Let's put the bias in this book right up front: We home school our children, speak about it enthusiastically and often, and encourage others to consider that choice. However, we do *not* believe home schooling is the best and automatic choice for everyone. We *do* believe that all parents should consider it carefully before saying either yes or no.

Over the years we have come to some general conclusions about parents.

Some parents won't home school. You may wind up in this group, and that could be either appropriate or unfortunate. It's *appropriate* if you consider all the alternatives and then conclude that home schooling is not a feasible or desirable option. But it's *unfortunate* if you are too comfortable with your current choice to even evaluate a potentially life-enhancing adventure or if you turn down the chance due to unfounded fears.

Some parents can't home school. You may want to home school, but can't find a way to make it work. You may be comforted to learn that there are legitimate reasons to turn away from home schooling even if you *really* want to do it.

Some parents shouldn't home school. Perhaps you aren't equipped, aren't committed, aren't matched to your children's personalities or aren't willing to pay the price of home schooling. If not, then we hope this book will acquaint you with the realities of home schooling and help point you to a more appropriate choice for your children.

But most parents can home school. The qualifications aren't as tough as you may think. The challenges aren't insurmountable. Parts of the task will be easier than you think, and parts will be harder. The difficulty of the task depends on who you and your children are—your lifestyle, your circumstances, your values, your beliefs and your convictions. The rewards depend on your motivation, your love, your resourcefulness and your commitment more than on your training and intelligence.

Many parents in this group try home schooling "just for a year or so to see if it works." Most never look back.

You want to know where you fit. So did we.

When we began to consider home schooling our children, there was little in print to help us make a responsible choice. Visits to the bookstores and libraries (and conventions) unearthed plenty of books on *how* to home school. And there were books detailing *reasons* to home school. But these seemed to be highly slanted, mentioning few (if any) drawbacks. Ultimately they failed to give us the balanced advice we felt we needed. There were books that advised against home schooling, but these too seemed to be unacceptably biased. We thought home schooling was probably a good thing to do, but we wondered if there were any deep, dark, ugly secrets that no one was willing to talk about.

We collected advice from our home-schooling friends (and from friends of those friends) and put it to use. When we finished deliberating, we chose home schooling for our children, then aged five and two. Our choice was not difficult, but we did not reach it all at once or without due process of deliberation. It grew on us as we considered it; we tried it and then tried it a little bit more . . . and now we wouldn't go back.

So we plunged into the adventure and found ourselves enjoying it more than we could have believed.

What made us think we could do it?

Are we special?

Yes and no.

We are unique, as all God's creatures are.

But we are still only a typical home-schooling family.

Elizabeth is at home full-time, but with several activities on the side. She does essentially all the schooling of our two children, Jennifer and Andrew. She is completing a degree through a correspondence course and is involved with local and church ministries. She takes in sewing jobs to earn extra money. But all these activities are ones that she can control. When things get busy, she does not accept any work for a while. And the correspondence course is done on her own timetable.

Dan works away from the home as an engineer and computer specialist, and also at home as a writer and technical services provider. He is the home school's "corporate sponsor," the principal, the main substitute teacher, the pitching coach, the science and advanced math adviser, and the teacher's main cheerleader.

We both have college degrees and are avid readers. We tend to be do-it-yourselfers. We are not psychologists, behavioral researchers or certified teachers. We are not educational specialists or child psychologists. Our teaching background is limited to Sunday-school classes and Bible studies.

Every day in home school has been a learning experience—for us as well as for the children. Experience creates survivors, survival cultivates wisdom, and wisdom draws questioners. Our enthusiasm for home schooling, as well as the success our children have experienced with it, have led people to seek our insight, opinions and advice. As we passed our accumulated wisdom on to others, we frequently heard the complaint that "there's nothing about this in the books out there."

Thus this book: a collection of the questions we had to answer for ourselves, as well as a compilation of ideas we have collected. The subject is not "how to home school"—there are many books to help you do that—but "how to decide if you *should* home school." Be warned that not we do not have all the answers. These questions and discussions are intended to help you examine the issues, understand the choices and their possible consequences and eventually find the answers that work for you and your family.

We have tried to be fair in handling our perceptions of the pros and cons of home schooling, and open about our personal experiences. Naturally, we use our family for many illustrations, and we hope that you enjoy these stories.

Additional tales and comments came from a survey we circulated among our friends and through the far-flung home-schooling network; we thank all who responded, and we have sprinkled some of their (anonymous) stories in quotes throughout the book.

We are committed Christians who are trying to apply God's Word to every area of our lives. We believe that since God has set us to the task of teaching our children at home, God is also equipping us for that task and is providing all the backup we need to complete that job.

Yet we do recognize that people consider home schooling for reasons other than spiritual or religious convictions, and perhaps some of our readers do not share our theology. We have tried to make this book helpful to you no matter what your personal spiritual convictions. But our belief that God has authority over all areas of our lives is an integral aspect of our discussion in this volume.

Ultimately, it is our sincere desire and prayer that this book may help you educate your child—whether you choose to do it yourself or to entrust your child's education to a school.

2

What Do You Mean by a Good Education?

Why do our children even need an education?
Society expects it.
The government demands it.
You want it.
But why?

The Weakness of Children

Children need an education because they are ignorant, immature and unskilled. They need to be carefully and patiently prepared to take their place in the world. This is a disturbing, fundamental and revealing truth.

Children are ignorant. Ignorance is not to be equated with stupidity. Ignorance is the lack of critical information and knowledge.

Someone has to teach children language, tell them the names of the colors, introduce them to the letters of the alphabet, define for them the boiling point of water and reconstruct for them the events that led to World War II. Someone has to inform them that there is a God, tell them that God made the heavens and the earth and relate for them the story of God's descent to earth in the form of Jesus to redeem us lost "sheep."

Children are immature. They are born helpless—physically and emotionally undeveloped and unaware of any world beyond the one of which they are the center. Someone has to teach them of the existence of other *persons* with needs, rights and responsibilities. Someone must teach them civility, manners, respect and obedience to authorities.

Coming to maturity involves turning facts and information into wisdom, self-control and respect for the value of other people (indeed, for everything God has made).

Children are unskilled. Children need skills to take their eventual place in society, yet they are born with none. Someone has to teach them to use their brains and their fingers wisely, coming to know or learning to do something that other people will find of value. People have an innate need to engage in meaningful and fulfilling activity, and they come under the universal curse of needing to secure food, clothing and shelter for themselves and their loved ones.

The Strength of Children
But there are matching strengths for these weaknesses; children are ready to learn, children are eager to imitate their heroes, and children are anxious to do things on their own.

Children are ready to learn. Why is a word learned early, not long after *mama* and *dada*. Just try to prevent children from learning! If you can't answer their questions, they'll ask someone else who can satisfy their need to know.

The world doesn't make sense to children, so they ask questions of people they trust in order to fit the answers into coherent pictures.

Children are eager to imitate their heroes. Children look up to their heroes and strive to be just like them. Dressing in their clothes, using their words, accepting their beliefs, trying to help with the tasks at hand—these are all forms of hero worship.

This can both exhilarating and frightening for parents. We are heroes who can teach bad things just as effectively as good things. Our children are little sponges that absorb every minute detail of what happens in the home. (It's humbling to hear a child repeat something that we just finished saying, especially in the same tone of voice!)

Children are anxious to do things on their own. "*Me* do it!" This protest greets any attempt to do for a child a task he considers both grown-up and within his abilities. Children strive to master the tasks that interest them, as fast as their understanding and physical powers allow, and they want the applause and approval that rightly follow a job well done.

It's interesting to see what the Bible says about the education and upbringing of the child Jesus: "And Jesus grew in wisdom and stature, and in favor with God and men" (Lk 2:52).

The method is not mentioned, but the results are. Jesus acquired knowledge, maturity and skill. He grew in wisdom—knowledge retained and properly applied. He grew in stature—taller and stronger—and learned to shoulder his social responsibility. He grew in favor with both God and people, for everything he did was seen to be good.

Trades stayed in the family, or rather families stayed in the trade; the carpenter's son would probably be a carpenter too. And where would he learn except at his father's side? Apprenticed not only in woodworking and craftsmanship but in humanity and humility and life.

And this is appropriate, for parents are the main interpreters of life for their children. "Daddy, what's this?" "Mommy, why . . . ?" We are the ones they turn to as they seek to make sense of their world; their dependence is both a privilege and a great responsibility. Deuteronomy 6:6-7 points out how parents are to teach God's laws to their children all day, every day, and in all activities: "These commandments that I give you today are to be upon your hearts. Impress them on your children. Talk about them when you sit at home and when you walk along the road, when you lie down and when you get up."

This kind of parent-child teaching is an integral component of life. Does this refer to instruction in reading and writing and math, geography and history and science? Or does it refer only to moral and spiritual education, and setting good examples for our children to follow?

The line is not easy to draw. How can children decipher the commands of God unless they can read? How can they practice fair trade and commerce unless they can count? How will they understand what God has done for them unless they are made aware of their history? How will they see God's hand in nature unless they inquire with a mind that has been trained to seek order and harmony and sense? And how will they work out the social and practical implications of their learning without the aid of those who are older and wiser?

The early schools in the United States were founded in this spirit: to teach all people to read the Word of God and the law of the land for themselves. The leaders of the newly formed country were held accountable to interpret God's laws and to enact earthly laws. Reading and understanding came first, and other endeavors followed naturally and logically.

Home schooling was widely practiced in the early years of the American nation. All four of the presidents depicted on Mount

Rushmore were home schooled or privately tutored. So were Americans Benjamin Franklin, Woodrow Wilson, Booker T. Washington, James Madison, Alexander Graham Bell, Robert E. Lee, Pearl S. Buck, Franklin Roosevelt, Martha Washington, John Quincy Adams and Thomas Edison, as well as Europeans Charles Dickens, John Wesley, Andrew Carnegie, Florence Nightingale, Wolfgang Amadeus Mozart and Agatha Christie.

Although public schools have come to be the norm in American society, many of us choose to teach our children in our homes. But what do we teach, and how?

We teach by example through our speech and conduct, our consideration for others, and the importance we give to Bible study and prayer. We demonstrate how to worship, how to run a household, how to celebrate, how to deal with stress and trouble, how to be ill, how to laugh, how to grieve and how to give our skill to our work. And whatever we teach, we must teach consistently and as an accurate reflection of God's truth.

The foundations of a child's education are laid in the home by the parents. But must *all* the learning take place within those walls?

We do believe that the parents *should* choose, direct (or oversee) and monitor that education. Help can come from friends and experts, but parents cannot abandon that final responsibility. Though they may delegate some of the tasks to others, they are ultimately responsible to determine the source, form and nature of the education their children receive. Parents do this best—not boards, not specialists, not committees and not even a village.

The purpose of educating children is (1) to create informed, mature, skilled people who interact properly with both society and God and (2) to fulfill their innate needs for reliable information, worthy heroes and lasting accomplishments. The question is, What methods will best achieve these goals?

Parents have multiple options in choosing what path to pursue.

3

What
Choices Do
You Have?

If you have school-age children now, you are probably the product of a public or a parochial school. But you are not limited to your own experience in considering the best way to fulfill your child's need for an education. We have developed a list of nine options for you to consider.

Public Schools

Public schools are the norm in North America. Adhering to this norm requires a minimum of effort, preparation, extra expense, frustration and deliberation, since "it's always been like this." Yet a review of U.S. history shows that Americans have employed a variety of methods in securing the proper education of their children; public schools as we know them are only a bit more than 150 years old, and are intrinsically no better or worse than other methods that were tried.

Nevertheless, the public schools are in trouble. The litany of problems is familiar:

"The schools aren't teaching the basics."

"All the good teachers have quit."

"They're busing kids too far across town."

"The halls and the playgrounds are dangerous."

"The kids are bored out of their minds."

"There are drugs and guns everywhere."

"The schools are run by the gangs."

"Today's graduates can't read, write or make change, but they know how to carry knives and use condoms."

Our local school system is in deeper trouble than most, and seldom does a day pass without an article in the newspaper detailing the current problems or the most recent proposed solutions.

There are, however, some very good public schools and some excellent teachers. Unfortunately, many of them may not talk of God in any concrete terms, and they must present evolution as a fact, not a theory. They must be careful about touching their students, either in affection or in discipline.

The main point is that public schools are run by the government—state or local. They are staffed by government employees, run to government standards, and overseen by individuals who are either elected or politically appointed to their posts. As a result, individual parents can influence—but not control—the selection of curriculum, the hiring and firing of teachers, and the general rules of the school.

Sending your children to public school is easy. It's right there and waiting, and your taxes have already paid for the teachers, the building, the equipment and facilities, and even the bus your kids ride. You will still have to pay for textbooks, paper supplies, clothes, lunches and other "necessities."

Some students do thrive in public schools. Young people who demonstrate leadership skills, resist being swayed by their peers, are competitive, excel in sports, function well in groups, like frequent change and need lots of activity may do well in a public school.

One parent who filled out our questionnaire had this to say: *We have placed our children in the local public school system because we wanted to take advantage of the many different sorts of programs they offered—and were unable to afford a private school. We are very involved in the schools our children attend, and several of their teachers have been Christians. We have been happy with our choice. We also believe that we are to be like salt and light to the world, and need to be out where the people are who need Jesus.*

Parochial Schools (Catholic or Protestant)

Parochial schools resemble public schools, except that the governing authority is a denominational church with varying degrees of formality and orthodoxy. They usually offer kindergarten through eighth grade; there may be a separate high school. Discipline is enforced. Dress codes are common, and uniforms may be mandatory. Religious instruction, including attendance at mass or daily services, is often compulsory. Teaching about God is integrated into the curriculum, even though the textbooks may come from secular publishers. The school is usually next door to the church and may share multipurpose facilities. Parents are generally expected to be very involved.

Your taxes haven't paid for this option, so tuition is extra. Parts of the operating cost are underwritten by the church; parochial schools are often cited as having good dollars-per-student ratios. Some schools are unable to provide extensive libraries, computer labs or other "extras" that are more readily available in the public schools. Music, art and shop classes may also be limited.

Must you attend the church in order to enroll your child in its school? No, although parish members may receive priority on the waiting list or may be eligible for lower tuition. (In some cases, you may receive a reduced rate if you enroll more than one child.)

A non-Catholic parent wrote,

I send my children to the local Catholic school because it is doing an excellent job of educating my children and teaching them God's principles. The school is friendly, the teachers are approachable, and my children have no difficulty in advancing.

Secular Private Schools

Private schools tend to be costly, but they sometimes offer a price break for a second or third child. Also, they may offer financial assistance or academic scholarships. These schools usually are populated with the children of financially well-off parents; the result is often a racially and economically unbalanced student body.

Most private schools maintain high academic and behavioral standards, and they may call for uniforms as part of the dress code. Traditionally, private schools do an excellent job of preparing students for college, as the following parent attests:

Our children are attending one of the best private schools in the area. We are able to afford it, and we definitely want to prepare our children to take their place as productive citizens. The school has excellent programs to meet an array of needs and interests, and we are grateful that God has allowed us this luxury. Since this option was open to us, we felt we should grasp it. We're not sure what God has in mind for our children, but this sort of educational foundation is sure to enable them to go wherever they want in life.

Again, extensive sports and arts opportunities may be limited.

Christian Private Schools

These private schools may be associated with a specific denomination, or they may be "independent." Many of them ask students and/or parents to sign a statement of faith, and most of them enforce a code of conduct. Chapel sessions may be held daily or weekly; religious teaching is a major part of the curriculum.

Just because a school is Christian does not mean that all the students are Christians. Some parents send their children to Christian schools because they have experienced behavioral problems at their other school and at home. The parents hope that the Christian influence will straighten their children out. (Some Christian schools have become known as dumping places for "bad kids.") Some parents expect a Christian school to shield their children from the problems of the outside world. This is not realistic. Christian schools also have many problems, but on a smaller scale.

Children who function well in a highly structured environment generally do fine in a Christian school. Many Christian schools use curricula that involve a lot of seatwork. Some children love this and thrive on it. Children who are restless may find it difficult to stay in one place for more than a few minutes and can come to be labeled as inattentive or troublesome.

The kind of environment offered by a Christian school may be good for some children, such as the child who needs individualized attention or is shy and tends to follow rather than lead. A new Christian or a child who has not yet made a commitment to Christ may also blossom here.

If the school's basic philosophy and its statement of faith are agreeable to you, and if you feel that you can work with the teachers, this may prove to be an excellent option for your children. Academic standards tend to vary. This may be a concern for you, depending on what you want your children to do after graduating from high school. Ask about this. Find out what most of the students do after graduation. Some of these schools do an excellent job of preparing their students for higher education. In the words of one parent:

We are unable to home school our children, and felt that the Christian school was the best option for us. Yes, it is expensive, but we willingly make the necessary sacrifices elsewhere. We are very pleased with the results: our eldest just went to college, and had no difficulty (academically or socially) jumping from a Christian school into a secular state college.

"Church" Schools

"Church" schools are smaller than private Christian schools, as they are generally associated with a particular church and are operated as an outreach to the members or the community. Staffs are small, and may be selected from the church membership rather than a pool of certified teachers. These qualities may be exactly what you want for your child, but be aware that some high schools and colleges will not accept such an institution as an entrance school for their programs.

These schools almost always enforce a dress and behavior code. Parents may be required to sign a doctrinal statement and may be expected to volunteer time and services to the school.

Many church schools offer only kindergarten through sixth or eighth grade. Being small helps make it easier to get to know the staff and other families, but it also might mean that the school does not have as much in the way of resources and options. The basics can be taught with a minimum of equipment, but middle and high schoolers will need access to science labs, computers and technical equipment—items that many church schools have difficulty fitting into a limited budget. The atmosphere in this sort of school may be more important to you than academic achievement, especially in the early years.

We are sending our child to the [elementary] school that is being held in our church building. It is small, and right now we really like the environment. Mom helps out regularly and that way feels she has the opportunity for input and observing the classes. We realize that as our child gets into the higher grades, we will have to choose another school, but we felt this was the best place for her to start.

One family that was involved in such a school pointed out that personal conflicts were more difficult to resolve with such a small staff:

In the end, we pulled our children out. The initial conflict between my older child and her teacher was never resolved; it only escalated, and there was no place to hide from the disapproval and divisiveness. Even Sundays were affected, because my child saw the same teacher at church.

Boarding Schools

Some families, notably missionaries or other families with long-term overseas commitments, have relied on boarding schools. The boarding school is essentially a private school with live-in students and staff. All aspects of the students' lives—school, recreation, housing, food and social life—are controlled by the school. All at a handsome price.

Boarding school seems to deny one of the most basic premises of the Christian family—being together to honor God in all the workings of the home and learning to get along with one another in rough as well as easy times. If one or more members of that family grow up somewhere else, that unity is not going to develop, and the family will have a much more difficult time working together.

Nevertheless, a boarding school may be a satisfactory solution in extreme situations. We heard of a father who suddenly lost his wife. His work schedule required extensive travel, and the family decided that a boarding school would be best until the father could find a job in town. Although being separated from their father at a painful time was not good for the children, they were used to his absence, and a reputable boarding school was preferable to other short-term arrangements.

A school administrator (of a secular private school) told us that when the parents of a problem middle-school student visit him seeking counsel, he sometimes advises a boarding school because he can see that the parents are a major part of the problem. He feels that the structure, discipline and forced independence of a boarding school may prove helpful to the child.

Correspondence/Electronic Schools

Completing courses through the mail is not a new concept; students of all ages and abilities in rural or isolated (especially missionary) settings have obtained degrees via the mail. Now the Internet and electronic on-line services are changing our entire culture, and education is not immune from its effects.

The primary benefits of the electronic universe are information and communication. Knowledge is available twenty-four hours a day (all you have to do is find it!), and people can reach each other almost instantaneously around the globe. The mail-order university is becoming the electronic university. Many families are relying on this sort of schooling for their high-school-age children:

I couldn't keep up with the things my stay-at-home high schooler was doing, so I quit trying. We are happy with his correspondence work. He loves the computer, and uses the Internet, so it's a natural match. It seems kind of impersonal to me, but it works for him.

Home Schools

A home is where a family lives, and a school is an institution for educating children or for giving instruction. Combined, they keep the educational process within the family.

The major distinctive of home schooling is that the parents have complete control of curriculum, structure, general rules of behavior and environment. The other schooling options offer parents only limited influence in these areas, at best.

Typically, one parent (usually Dad) works full-time while the other parent (usually Mom) does the bulk of the teaching. She may hold a part-time job or engage in a cottage industry for supplemental income.

The division of labor is quite flexible, varying with work circumstances and personal abilities. If Dad is home every night, it will be easier for him to be regularly involved in the schooling of his little ones (or not-so-little ones). Some dads spend an hour two nights a week working on advanced math with their high schoolers. Others love to get involved in the area of science, and do experiments one evening a week.

And there are other dads whose involvement is basically limited to supporting the whole operation (financially and emotionally), asking how things are going and showing the children how to use the computer. It can be misleading to label parents "teaching" or "nonteaching." Schooling proceeds twenty-four hours a day, led by whoever is in charge at the moment, even though the formal academics are generally confined to a specific time slot, as the following parent suggests:

We are home schooling together, as a family, and truly benefiting from that. The children really are best friends to each other. We know exactly what they are doing in school, and are able to oversee their relationships outside the family more easily. Academically, the children are doing outstanding work, and we are not held back by the lowest-common-denominator standards they would encounter in a classroom. We love the flexibility, too! We've been

able to make our vacations "school trips," and by traveling off-season we save a lot of money.

Teachers can be drawn from the extended family as well. We have been direct beneficiaries of the attention and interest given by our children's grandfather. He is able to visit our children almost every week, and over the years he has been involved in teaching them math and the history of our state. He has also been involved in field trips and outings.

We are jealously preserving the time our children have to spend with their grandparents, aware that the time will come when our parents will not be as well or as strong as they are now to take as active a role in their grandchildren's lives. We want our children to know our parents. Now is the time to do it. Activities can be as simple as reading special books together. They can involve taking short trips together to research or visit places of interest. If it is at all possible to include your parents in your child's education, we would encourage you to do so. Everyone will benefit, and your child will never forget those special times.

There are home-schooling families who, for a price, will teach your children with theirs. However, this arrangement would not produce the benefits of home schooling simply because you are not the one doing it. And your children would still be in a different environment for academics than for everyday learning and activities. However, this has proven to be a workable solution for some families, and may be worth closer examination on your part. It does offer your children a very good teacher-student ratio. How do you find such a family? Ask the home-schooling families you know or contact your county home-schooling repre-sentative.

Some home-schooling families hire a tutor to work with their children in subjects that they are not familiar with or when their children want to go further than the parents can lead. This could

be a high-school or college student who is a whiz in a particular
area.

The "Combo" Approach

The schooling options we have presented so far are not irrevoca-
ble. You have the freedom to switch from one option to another
or to combine approaches within your family. Who says all of the
kids have to do the same thing?

There are home-schooling families who are not teaching all of
their children at home. Some stay at home to do their studies
while their brothers or sisters go off to the local school. In these
situations the parents have carefully assessed the needs of their
children, recognizing that they are different people, and have
tried to place each child in the learning environment that is
optimal for that individual.

Some families like to have their children in a couple of
different schools throughout their elementary and high-school
years. They feel that exposure to a variety of people and approaches to education is a worthwhile learning process in and of
itself. It is excellent discipline for children to learn to get up at
the same time each morning, catch the bus to school, experience
the "classroom" setting, feel the restrictions of working with
twenty or so other students, and discover that they cannot always
have the teacher's undivided attention. Children could also benefit from a few years of home schooling, learning self-study habits,
completing solo projects and working with people of different
ages and backgrounds.

*We are trying to place our children in the schooling option that
works for them as individuals, so that means home school for two,
public school for another, and a Christian school for the fourth. I
do feel divided when schedules conflict with each other, but so far
we're coping.*

Such an arrangement bears great resemblance to the working world. Adults are not segregated by age, all doing the same task in the same way at the same time.

Narrowing the Options

None of these educational choices are inherently right or wrong, though the availability, quality and affordability of each option will vary from place to place. The trick is to figure out which ones work best for your family.

4

What Are the Right Questions?

Being faced with so many options can be perplexing. Where do you start? Which option will work best in helping your children achieve literacy and self-sufficiency?

For every option that interests you, ask all the relevant questions you can think of. Ask them of yourself, of other parents, of the people responsible for the schools in question. Ask the students too! We will provide you with some sample questions, but you must provide your own answers!

What does God want for your children? Go back to the purpose of education and consider what your responsibilities and priorities are. You may be familiar with the "line of priorities" that Christians are urged to adopt: God is first, mate and children are second, job and church come next. The problem with this analysis is that it separates God from the rest of life. We don't believe God intended it to be that way. And it is virtually impossible to allot our time so precisely. Rather, we believe that God wants to be involved in everything we do: "Whatever you do, work at it with all your heart" (Col 3:23). This verse means to pursue "heartily" whatever educational option you choose for your children. What school option we choose is not intrinsically more or less holy than another choice. It is how we live out that choice that has the potential to be holy.

What is your philosophy of education? Write it out. This exercise is not always easy to do, but it does cause you to think, and it will help you evaluate the approach of any school you may be considering.

What is the school's philosophy of education? Most private and parochial schools clearly articulate their philosophy of education and are willing to respond to questions you may have about it. It may be more difficult to get a clearly defined statement of philosophy from a public school, depending on the school system. In fact, this is likely to be a primary area of conflict with any public school system.

Does the school's philosophy line up with what the Bible teaches about families? Does it teach what you want your children to learn? Is it consistent with what you believe about life?

What are the teachers like? Do the teachers listen to the parents? Do they invite your involvement? Are they Christians? Are they accepting of a Christian worldview? To what extent does the school board dictate or limit teaching about religion and morality?

What textbooks does the school use? Are they compatible with your worldview? Are they sturdy, quality books? Inquire about book fees. Do you buy or rent the books? Can they be resold later?

Would your children be safe? Talk to other parents and to the local police. They may be more willing to share crime-related information than the school itself.

What is peer pressure like at the school? This will depend greatly on your child's personality and the social dynamics of the school. However, some schools are able to teach the strength of diversity and draw students away from the cookie-cutter mentality. Peer pressure can be just as intense at a church school as at a secular school.

Is there anything in the school environment that can adversely affect my children? It is nearly impossible to foresee every possible problem, but if you have any doubts, big or small, consider them to be warning flags and prayerfully consider what they could mean. Your sense of doubt may indicate that God wants you to take a closer look at something. Children who attend even a Christian school will not be isolated from prejudice, pride, angry outbursts, poor leadership, gossip or injustice. These sins permeate society, including our churches and our homes.

How willing are you to be stretched? How willing are you to learn more about the learning process and to get intimately involved in your child's educational experience? Many home-schooling parents comment on how much they are learning, and how their little children know as much or more than they do about our solar system (outer space) or digestive tract (inner space). We parents then joke that we actually home school for our own educational benefit.

What about our responsibility to contribute to society, to be salt in a world that is morally decaying? Should you and your children be "making a difference" in a secular school or be "hiding away" in a protected environment? Many public schools are crying out for more parents to be involved. If the majority of them were Christians, just think what sort of influence they could have! A godly grandmother expressed her concern to us:

If every Christian family home schooled, there would be very little

*influence for godliness in the public or private schools. That's what
I don't like about home schooling—your family loses an excellent
opportunity to be a witness in the school system.*

She is correct in her observation. But does her application apply
to everyone? Which comes first? Am I gambling with my children's spiritual and moral well-being by allowing them to be
schooled by and with people who do not honor God?

In his book *Choosing Your Child's School,* David W. Smith
discusses our saltiness as Christians, suggesting that parents who
choose to keep their children out of public schools do so out of
fear. They are not fulfilling our Lord's directive to go into all the
world, teaching and making disciples. This may be the case for
some, but we have difficulty saying this is true across the board.
Still, this thought-provoking book is well worth the reading.

A family we know felt pressured to home school. When they
mentioned that they were considering enrolling their daughter
in the local public school, their friends were flabbergasted. But
this family had considered the issue prayerfully and felt that this
child, at this point in time, belonged in the local school. They
knew some of the teachers, and they had heard that the principal
encouraged parental involvement. They wanted the Lord to use
them to make a difference in the school.

We personally are not (at this time) willing to lay our children's
education and well-being on the line in exchange for an opportunity to make a difference in our local schools. One reason is
that our gifts lie elsewhere. God has given us areas of ministry
that do not involve the politics of persuasion or committee
service, and we don't feel that we can neglect our current responsibilities to get involved in a task for which we are not equipped.

*Do you have reason to believe that your children's attendance at
this school would contribute to poor behavior, poor attitudes or
inadequate academic performance?* What do you see in the chil-

dren who have attended this school?

My daughter occasionally spends three or four hours at the home of a little friend who attends public school. When she returns home, she is surly and rude—nothing like my sunny, polite child. If she picks up such bad behavior after four hours with one child, how would she act after living with a classroom of kids six hours a day five days a week? I'm glad I home school her!

To which leaders are you exposing your children? Will the teachers and other people your child comes into contact with set a good example? Will they be good mentors for your child? Might he pick up attitudes, beliefs and mannerisms from the teachers that you do not find acceptable?

Do you like the "products" of the school? Are they literate, sociable, reliable? One of the things that attracted us to home schooling was the kids' behavior. We have met remarkably few home-schooled teens who weren't bright, personable, confident and surprisingly polite.

How much will this cost? What does everything add up to, including tuition, room, board, food, books, lab supplies, field trips, team fees, club dues and other incidentals? Is financial aid available?

Is there a dress code? Can you afford it? Can you live with it? Will your children be able to live with it? Will it save or cost you money?

Is there a statement of faith? Do you agree with it? Would you be able to explain and defend it to other parents?

How big are the classes? What is the teacher-pupil ratio? Will your child receive enough instruction and attention?

What is the school facility like? Is it an environment you want your children to be in for thirty or more hours a week? Is it attractive? Is it clean? Is it spacious enough for the activities that take place in it? Is it safe? What about the equipment and furnishings? What do the kitchen and cafeteria and restrooms look like? Is the art on the walls authorized? Do the teachers and pupils take pride in their surroundings?

What was your schooling experience like? How has it affected your goals for your children? Just because you may have had a great (or terrible) time does not mean that your children will too. They may be very different from you, and schools have changed drastically in the past twenty-five years.

What do you envision for your children's academic career? How far in school do you want your children to go? Will the education your children receive enable them to contribute to society and support themselves and their future families? Are technical schools or colleges part of the plan?

Will you be happier with your children if you keep them at home? Do you have concerns about your children's being in a school environment every day? Do you have reason to believe that this may not be best for them?

Do you believe that children should be taught as much as possible early on? Should children grow and develop at their own pace? Or should they be encouraged on to bigger and better accomplishments? Raymond and Dorothy Moore's *Better Late Than Early* and Doreen Claggett's *Never Too Early* give opposing views on the question. See the resources section of this book for details.

Do your children have any special needs? Is the school willing to work with any special needs your child may have?

Do you want your children to learn a foreign language or to receive special encouragement in art, science or athletics? Will the schooling option you choose make this possible? Do you have reason to believe that your child has gifts in a certain area? Do you want to focus on that?

How important is a Bible-based curriculum that includes accurate biblical teachings? Perhaps you feel that the religious instruction you provide at home is adequate, and you are mainly looking for a solid academic curriculum. If you want specifically Bible-oriented materials to be used for teaching, then check out the materials used by any possible school carefully.

Is the type of discipline and training employed by the school consistent with what your children are learning at home? If not, will your children be confused by experiencing different approaches to discipline?

How willing are you to participate in fundraisers and other corporate school activities? Do you have a moral objection to selling raffle tickets? Would you want to help sponsor a Halloween party? What do you believe about the children's doing fundraising? Do you want yours involved? Ask how funding is obtained, and what sort of fundraisers you might have to be involved in.

Are you willing to volunteer some of your time to help coach, monitor or mentor at school? Will you be required to help out? What sort of skills can you offer? Will you be able to assist on a regular basis if necessary?

Are you a joiner, a loner or a do-it-yourselfer? Do you prefer to do things on your own, at your own speed, in your own space? Or do you love to be with other people, exchanging ideas and interacting on many levels? Being a do-it-yourselfer is not a requirement for home schooling, but it does make some aspects of it a little easier. You may have fewer contacts with other families if you home school. Good or bad, this issue should be taken into consideration.

Are you a leader or a follower? Do you depend on the people around you to show you the way? Do you need to be shown the way to go, or do you like to find it for yourself?

Whatever choice you make, will you be satisfied that you did your very best to provide your children a quality education with the tools that God has made available to you? Although you can adjust your choices as you go and switch your plans along the way, this is not an experiment you can redo from the beginning if the final results are not acceptable.

Any more questions?

If home schooling still looks attractive to you, read on. The following chapters address specific questions commonly asked about home schooling.

5

Whose Idea Was This, Anyway?

We all experience pressure from the people and the events in our lives, and we all deal with it differently. Some of us are able to resist it just because we are stubborn. Some of us succumb to pressure easily because we are people pleasers.

What particular pressure has led you to think about home schooling? For some it may be a general dissatisfaction with the schools, in terms of academic, moral and safety concerns. For others it may be a spiritual conviction.

Is it your idea to pursue home schooling for your child? A parent who is not convinced of the value of home schooling will find it difficult to home school well or enthusiastically. Such ambivalence will also be communicated to the child.

Right and Wrong Pressures

Some families have felt pushed into home schooling by persistent pressure from families at church who express their belief loudly and often that "since you're a Christian and since you love your child, of course you'll home school."

It is hard to stand up against a whole roomful of people, especially when these people are ones you worship with and spend time with—your friends, your family in Christ. It is easy to be made to feel "unspiritual" when all these successful, outgoing home-schooling families are telling you it's the only thing to do. On the other hand, some churches have few home schoolers and view them as well-intentioned but uncomfortably far to the right of the beaten path.

"Everybody's doing it" is just as poor a reason for adults as it is for children. But home schooling "just to be different" is not sound either. Some people home school because God has shown them that they should. They may still have questions, but their obedience stems from a desire to love and honor the Lord. Some may feel pressured into home schooling out of dissatisfaction with their local public schools. Others may have limited budgets that preclude private schooling or tutoring options. Others may feel that it is their *only* option; they live in isolated areas or have special-needs children.

It may be difficult to walk the fine line of listening to other people's ideas and input without automatically giving in to or automatically objecting to what they suggest. We all need input from our parents and in-laws, our close friends and relatives. The issue of home schooling has sparked many family debates. If this is the case for you, it may just be best to tell people after you have made a decision, and that's that. But if in the past you have found the feedback from these people to be helpful and godly, then take the time to listen to it now. It may not change your decision, but it may help you identify some fears or concerns lurking in the corners of your mind.

We were curious about home schooling. What we knew about it did not violate anything we knew in the Word of God; we had seen good results in families we knew; we did not know any reason (other than laziness and lack of self-confidence) that would prevent us from actually doing this; we were willing to try; we realized that we were already teaching our children. After praying about it, we felt peaceful about trying it, with the idea that we would take one year at a time and regularly review our progress.

We cannot say that we ever felt specifically convicted that home schooling was irresistibly God's will for us and that not doing so would have amounted to disobedience. We felt it was something that God gave us the freedom to choose.

And we chose it *together.*

Unity in Parenting

Are you and your mate in agreement in regard to the educational alternatives you have? *A word of caution: if you and your spouse cannot agree about home schooling, we strongly recommended that you consider another option.*

> *The idea of teaching my children at home appealed to me immensely, but my husband did not share my enthusiasm. He wasn't merely indifferent; he was thoroughly against it, but agreed to let me work with the children during the summer months. I loved it and wanted to continue, but he didn't want me to consider it any further. I felt rebellion boiling up inside me, but decided that it was more important to show our children a healthy marriage than it was to home school them.*

Usually Mom does the day-to-day teaching. But if she does not have her husband's support, their marriage can suffer tremendously. A troubled marriage shakes the entire home, and children are the innocent victims. If God wants you to home school, it will be evident to both partners. Of course, one partner can always refuse to listen to God. By the same token, if God does not want you to home school, you will feel unity in that decision. The decision does not necessarily come easily, especially if you are being pressured by others.

Some women find that their husbands are excited about the idea of home schooling but do not really feel up to the effort necessary to make it a reality in their home. After all, it's easy for him to endorse the choice because he is not the one who has to make it work on a day-to-day basis. She may feel that she is being forced into doing something that God has not called her to do. Or she may just not want to do it but may be hesitant to communicate this reluctance to her husband. Home schooling can't be successful without the wife's full support. It is a "whole couple" decision.

This is a decision to be reached on your knees, over a period of time. Don't make a snap decision. If you and your mate have differing opinions about home schooling, consider it a yellow flag. Take the time to discuss and explore. Talk with home-schooling families and with families in the schools under consideration. You may be able to talk with couples who also experienced disagreement in order to find out how they resolved it. If you want to home school but your mate does not, then you need to back off. Assure your mate that solidarity in your relationship comes first and that you are willing to consider other options. Work on it as a team.

Unity should extend to more than agreement in principle. One mother mentioned to us that her husband supported the idea of home schooling but actually did very little to help. She felt disappointed and overwhelmed by the responsibility of selecting the curriculum, preparing it, teaching it and providing supplementary materials. This situation resulted from a difference in personality types. The mother was a retiring person, letting her husband initiate most family activities and projects. But the father was a classic type A personality—enthusiastic, full of ideas, and very engrossed in his promising new business. He talked about what they could do for school but in reality did not have time to put into it. She thought that he had meant that he would do it, whereas he was just sharing some ideas.

The lesson here? Think about differences of opinion on which you and your mate have trouble communicating. Unless those differences are something that the two of you can agree to disagree on and are committed to working on with each other, they can lead to major difficulties.

Sometimes my husband was home when I was teaching the children, and he would be in the room or just wandering through. He would overhear what we were doing and insert what he thought were helpful pointers and ideas. In reality it frustrated me because it distracted my child, sometimes got us off the main point, and made me feel like he was second-guessing my work as a teacher. Besides, he hadn't even read the material, and didn't necessarily know where I was going! At first I just tried to ignore it, but soon realized that I would have to discuss it with him because I felt that I was being put down in front of the children.

Home schooling can be the tool God uses to get you and your mate to work on rough areas of your marriage. It will help expose those spots. Every family has difficulties. We all are sinners, and sin complicates relationships and really complicates communication. The next time you see a picture-perfect family (home schooling or not), try to remember that they are not perfect. They have faults and weaknesses too. They may be more mature and better equipped to deal with problems as they arise, but if God can work in their lives, God can do the same in yours!

The urge to home school can arise in any member of the family. However, the decision to home school, as well as the commitment to see it through, must be shared by both parents.

6

What Will
Your Day
Be Like?

Typical home-schooling days, like typical home-schooling families, are never the same. Our days change as the children grow and change, and as we adjust our curriculum. Hence the need for flexibility.

From Elizabeth's point of view, a schooling day starts around 8:30 a.m. By that time everyone has generally accomplished the morning routine of washing, dressing, tidying their rooms and having breakfast, not necessarily in that order. She and the children try to have family devotions at breakfast, but if that doesn't happen, they aim for dinner. At some point Elizabeth usually pops a load of laundry into the washer (the laundry room is next to the kitchen), loads the bread machine, kisses her husband off to work and perhaps makes a quick phone call. Her first official act is to turn on the telephone answering machine. She would have a hard time doing school without it, since it gives her the freedom to ignore the outside world or to at least control the intrusions it makes into the school day.

She starts Jennifer with her math lesson. That means sitting down with her, working through the lesson and practicing a few problems before assigning the work for the day. Meanwhile Andrew is doing his piano practicing and occasionally a music theory assignment. He also uses this time to go over his Scripture memory verses for Sunday school.

Once Jennifer is off and running, Elizabeth shifts her focus to Andrew. It's usually about 9 a.m. by now. They do his spelling lesson and a language arts lesson, and she assigns any corrections from his spelling or writing work. Sometimes she can assign his math lesson or a few workbook pages before she gets back to check Jennifer's math work and discuss her corrections. She assigns another subject for Jennifer after going over the material and then goes to Andrew, doing the same for him and getting back to check on Jennifer and help with corrections. She does corrections on the spot with the child where possible. It reinforces the lesson, and they can deal with any problem right away while it is fresh in their minds.

Elizabeth may get pulled away from one child because the other has a question, but as the children are getting older she tells them that they have to honestly try a question or problem three times on their own before they may ask her for help.

Sometimes one child listens in on the other's reading lesson, just to have a break. Then they all snuggle up on the couch (under a big blanket if it's cold) and enjoy the story. The children are always ready to help with each other's science projects and sometimes participate in the other's drawing and art assignments.

Usually Elizabeth finishes up with having Andrew do flash cards and checking his penmanship. Some days he is assigned a composition, art project or computer work; he does the assignment on his own for her to look over later. When he focuses on his work, he's almost always finished by 11 a.m.

As Andrew finishes up, Elizabeth directs Jennifer through her history or geography, and they have great discussions on why, where, who, how, when and what. By 11:30, she is usually working on the assignments from her lessons, and Elizabeth is finished with teaching as such. Jennifer keeps working until her tummy signals for lunch; anything left over becomes home-work—finishing her math, writing a composition or copying out her science and history vocabulary. The children have about an hour free to eat, read and relax. They like to watch *Magic School Bus* when it's on the public broadcasting channel.

It takes about four hours for Jennifer to accomplish her daily work, and about two hours for Andrew. Of course, all that is subject to bad moods, head colds, distractions (of various sizes, colors and life forms) and difficulty in a particular subject. Some days are smoother than others.

Elizabeth's mornings are packed, but she does not plan to accomplish anything else during those hours; she just blocks them off for school. She had to learn this for herself. When the children had to spend only an hour or two doing their school-work, it was easy to get some other things done in the morning. As they grew and had more work to do, she still wanted to get things done in the mornings and wasn't able to do a good job on any of it. Finally she realized that mornings were for teaching, and only for teaching.

But some household tasks can be worked in, especially if they are in the kitchen. Sometimes, when both children are occupied, she finds time to make a phone call. She has done all facets of laundry while discussing the outline for a composition or the results of a science experiment. She can clean out the fridge, water the plants, sweep the floor or wipe away sticky handprints while discussing Jacksonian democracy. She does not have to be sitting down beside the children all the time. She purposely avoids too much of that in order to encourage them to work through problems on their own before turning to her. Sometimes Mom is too accessible!

But she does make sure each child has her focused attention at the beginning of the lesson. Once she is sure they are doing the work correctly, she can move away.

So what happens when an emergency arises (such as their geriatric cat's needing to see the vet at 10:15)? They adapt as well as they can. They do as much work ahead of time as they can on the nonportable stuff, and then they take their reading and workbook assignments in the car. (They can also recite memory verses or help one another with flash cards.) Anything over-looked will be finished up in the afternoon.

The frustrating situations involve the plumbers or other work-men who can only come in the mornings. If they have to work in the kitchen, the children move to another room, but Elizabeth still has to be available to them to answer questions or make decisions about the job. But that sort of thing doesn't happen often. There may be one or two of those disaster days every school year.

Elizabeth tries to avoid having other people in the house during the mornings; this includes not only repairmen but neighbors, relatives, sewing clients and roving salespersons. If the family has houseguests, she explains that she is busy in the mornings and is not available to entertain them. Even Dad can be a distraction if he stays home unexpectedly and gets in the way of the program!

After lunch (depending on the day of the week) they have piano or violin lessons, perhaps a swimming lesson or an outing for errands (groceries, bank, post office, new shoes, library).

Jennifer is responsible for doing her music practicing sometime during the rest of the day. If it's nice outside, the kids go out to play. If it's not nice, they can play on the computer or read or play with their other toys.

Sometimes Elizabeth likes to stay home to do some cleaning or get a start on dinner or baking. This is also when she does her own schoolwork and her sewing. She does not have much time to pursue her own friendships, and sometimes she feels lonely.

Every other Friday Elizabeth, Jennifer and Andrew meet with three other families to enjoy mutual support and to conduct some group activities. Field trips, crafts and games are the attraction of the day. All are connected to discussions and mini-lectures based on the biblical character quality studies of the KONOS curriculum.

Elizabeth truly cherishes her freedom to be at home with her children, teaching them, sharing their days with each other. Being a homemaker is what she always wanted to do, and she revels in it—most of the time!

But our way is not the only way:

☐ *We usually don't home school in the mornings ourselves. Most of ours is done in the afternoon, when the baby is napping.*

☐ *We don't ring the first school bell until after lunch, and classes continue after dinner when Dad is home to speak algebra to them or help them complete a project.*

Other families do their schoolwork throughout the entire day, with plenty of free time to handle unplanned adventures ("distractions") and explore interesting tangents. Setting the proper schedule is an ongoing process that is subject to change. However, overall consistency is definitely a plus in getting everybody smoothly through the day. The important part is making the format serve the goal of educating the children; the product is more important than the method.

7

Will You
Have to Fight
City Hall?

Are legal problems common in home schooling in the United States? No.

Are they possible? Yes.

Legal challenges are rare, but they can be complicated, painful and expensive if they occur. Most challenges to home schooling come from local public school officials, and they are generally based on several points of misunderstanding.

First, the authorities may not be aware of the legality, the actual nature and the benefits of home schooling. Such ignorance (or false information) tends to breed resistance, fear, suspicion and hostility.

Second, officials may assume that their power over public school children extends to those who are not enrolled. According to the law in some states, home schoolers are supposed to be registered with the local school boards, and sometimes those school boards do oversee curriculum. However, most school boards have established requirements and guidelines that they call "regulations"; these requirements are *not* necessarily law, and they may *not* be legally binding on home-schooling families.

Third, principals and school boards may understandably view the home-schooling family as a threat to their established way of life. Public schools have had little serious competition until recently, and they may not welcome the alternatives with open arms. In addition, certain public education interest groups have an open agenda of consolidating and controlling all educational activities; these groups will not look favorably on your interest in home schooling.

What happens when a parent withdraws a child from school? School officials are concerned that the child is being illegally or inadequately taught at home. A neighbor, relative or health-care worker reports to the school or child protection agency that a child is "not in school." Truant officers or child welfare officials then show up at the door, demanding to examine the child or the school environment. Accusations may be made, and charges may be filed. *But the law is the bottom line* for both home-schooling families and public officials.

Home Schooling Is Legal
Home schooling is legal in every part of the United States (and in most places around the world) as long as established conditions are met. The state applies the restrictions of its choice to the circumstances in which home schooling is conducted. This is an important distinction, for what the state requires may be less than what the local school board wants.

The chart below is a *general* summary of the relative ease of home schooling in the fifty states. Precise classification is impossible, since laws change frequently, and states with similar rules may enforce them with differing levels of tolerance and vigor. In addition, districts or counties may be more or less stringent than their state as a whole.

This chart is adapted from information supplied by the Home School Legal Defense Association and describes the various levels of requirements and regulations imposed on home-schooling families. Category 1 is the easiest, and category 5 is the most restrictive. Some of the states have been ranked by the political climate as well as standards and requirements. (This chart is subjective, is not legal advice and is subject to change.)

CATEGORY	STATES
Category 1 Few or no restrictions on home schooling. No teacher qualification/certification required. Student testing not required. Attendance records may be required. Little or no interaction with public school officials.	Arizona Idaho Illinois Indiana Mississippi Missouri Montana New Jersey Oklahoma Texas Wisconsin Wyoming
Category 2 Student testing or evaluation required in some situations. No teacher certification required.	Alabama Alaska California Colorado Delaware Florida Hawaii Kansas Kentucky Louisiana Michigan Minnesota Nebraska North Carolina Oregon Utah

Category 3 Student testing or annual portfolio review required. Teacher certification required in some situations.	Connecticut Georgia Maryland New Hampshire New Mexico Ohio South Carolina South Dakota Virginia Washington
Category 4 Student testing or annual portfolio review required. Teacher certification required.	Arkansas Iowa Maine Nevada New York Rhode Island* Tennessee Vermont West Virginia
Category 5 Tightest restrictions on home schooling. Teacher certification required. Frequent or annual student testing required.	Massachusetts North Dakota Pennsylvania

*Each school district of Rhode Island sets its own policy.

The Law Protects Families

The law, properly applied and enforced, protects you against unlawful entry and unreasonable interference. *You are not required to let any official into your home without a properly executed search warrant.* If you are challenged about your schooling arrangements, request a meeting in the challenger's office or a neutral location. Allowing these people into your home without a proper warrant is a mistake that can expose you to a bewildering variety of charges, from child neglect to public health violations. The intricacies of the law can be used against you if you are not properly prepared and defended.

Home School Legal Defense Association

The HSLDA is the first and best line of defense for home-schooling families who are challenged by government officials. They actively represent cases throughout the country and have an excellent track record. The vast majority of legal challenges are successfully resolved through their early intervention. No member family has been forced to stop home schooling, no member family has had children removed from the home, and no member parent has ever been sentenced to jail.

The HSLDA has also pursued federal civil rights actions and has assisted state home-schooling organizations with legislative battles within their home states. They attempt to educate the educators, stopping conflict before it can start.

Membership in the HSLDA allows families to home school free from the fear of facing legal threats alone. For $100 a year (or perhaps a little less if you have a membership in a recognized support group) you have full access to their expertise. *They do not charge any of their members for their legal services.*

The Good News
Some school boards welcome home schoolers and make selected after-school programs, special labs and lectures, field trips, team sports and libraries available for their use. Talk about teamwork! Sometimes this policy is established by a particular school on an individual basis, and sometimes it is followed by an entire school system. It doesn't hurt to ask; perhaps your local school has never been approached and would be open to considering your children's involvement. *On the whole, if you know your local law, meet its requirements and draw on the legal information and resources available to you, you will be left to home school in peace.*

Home Schooling Outside the United States
Laws outside the U.S. borders vary widely, and you need to

consult a legal expert for advice in regard to your specific area.

The resources section of this book lists legal information sources for Canada as well as general contacts for England, Japan, Germany, New Zealand, Puerto Rico and military bases overseas. Missionary families considering home schooling should also contact their mission boards and the American consul offices in their assigned countries.

8

Are You Qualified to Home School?

A neighborhood librarian once expressed her concern to us. "So who are these home-schooling parents anyway? Are they certified teachers? What are they teaching their children? How can they know that their children are learning what they need to learn?"

"We are home-schooling parents," we told her. "No, we are not *certified* teachers, but we are *qualified*. We are using time-tested methods and materials, and we have access to a great variety of materials that we select for each child individually. We can test our children, and in discussions with other parents, we can see that our children are doing just fine."

We also explained to her that home-schooling parents are highly motivated by the realization that they are responsible for their children's education; if they don't do a good job, it reflects poorly on them, and they will have only themselves to blame.

"We believe in God, but that's not why we're teaching our children at home. We know that we are able to do a better job with academics. The schools aren't getting the job done in a way that satisfies us."

It's easy to blame schools for doing a poor job because no one person has to step forward and take responsibility for shoddy workmanship. Parents blame the administrators, the administrators blame the teachers and the teachers blame the parents.

Being certified does not make a teacher effective; it does not automatically ensure that your child will learn. Educators have told us that certification is not necessarily a tough process. The courses themselves may concentrate more on administrative processes and crowd control than on effective teaching methods and dealing with special-needs and gifted children. Nor do teachers have to earn outstanding grades. They may barely scrape by, and then find themselves teaching your child a subject that they perhaps know little about. Certification does not make anyone a good teacher; it means that he or she has taken the required number of courses and has received a passing grade.

Certification is a matter of familiarity with methods of teaching and does not necessarily concern itself with whether the teacher knows the subject material or enjoys working with children in the first place. Nevertheless, teacher certification is required of home schoolers in some states, as noted in the previous chapter.

Dan doesn't particularly enjoy "working with children" in general, but he enjoys doing things with our children and some of their friends, who have become our friends as well. His best teachers were those who cared passionately about their subject material and sought to ignite that same passion in their students. These teachers also treated the students as individual persons with rights and responsibilities, not nameless, faceless subhumans to be dragged through a syllabus and shoved out the door as "trained" or "educated."

Fears and Doubts

Qualification can be a matter of fighting doubts, facing fears and making commitments. What are your fears—deep, silent, hidden fears whose existence you don't like to admit, even to yourself? Fears related to self-confidence seem to surface when people start talking about home schooling. Realizing that we have taken on the task of educating our children can be scary. But we assumed this task when they were conceived, not when they reached kindergarten age.

Numerous sermons, books and prayers try to help us deal with our fears. Fear is a side effect of sin that holds us back from trying new things. Can you identify your fears? An objective friend may be able to help you. Write them out so that you can see them in black and white. Pray over them. Talk to home-schooling parents, or any parents whose opinions you respect. If you are as flawed as we are, you know from experience that some days you just feel fearful. Other days you cope better. That is part of being human, and it's a great comfort to realize that God delights in using very frail humans to accomplish great tasks. Take some time to read about people who played a role in the Old Testament.

The Bible commands us over and over again not to be afraid. Feeling concern in the face of situations that we are uncertain about should drive us to our knees in prayer, not leave us wringing our hands in despair.

What Are the Most Common Fears?

Some people fear they are not patient or loving enough to teach their children well. And they are probably right! We all need to be changed in some area or another. (Did you think home schooling would reshape just your kids?) Do you struggle with being impatient? Home schooling may be the agent God uses to teach you more patience.

Some parents fear they will end up quitting part way through the school year. It's not necessarily good for children to observe their parents giving up, but the effort may not be as draining as you think. (Besides, is it wrong to abandon a project that is *not* working? Part of our maturity is demonstrated by our ability to acknowledge failure and move on.)

To be perfectly honest, there are many times we have felt overwhelmed and even afraid of what lies ahead of us in our home-schooling efforts. We think about the increased load of subjects as the children get older, and a sense of panic sometimes threatens to overwhelm us. We have learned that what we feared about subject materials and requirements for grade four (when our daughter was only in grade one) was unfounded. We are growing with our children! Our daughter is now capable of doing more and more of her work without anyone hovering nearby. She starts an assignment, and we check it partway through. When it is finally done, we work on corrections together. Back in grade one, she would not have been able to work that way. Parents of high-school students tell us that their children do almost all of their work by themselves. Talk about self-discipline! By this stage, most of what the parent does is help prepare reading lists and outlines for studies and generally oversee the work.

It's hard to quit when you know it may be difficult to enroll your child in a good school halfway through the year. This is a good reason to make a commitment to see a year through.

Some people fear that they don't know enough to teach their children. Consider home schooling an opportunity to continue your own education, or to supplement it. We have learned more than our children have since we started home schooling. We have had the opportunity to read the books that were never included in our formal education. We have had the opportunity to explore things much more fully than we ever could before. We have learned about teaching, and have come to know our children even better. We know more about motivating them. We know ourselves better, and are enjoying our second education. In having to teach the basics to little ones, we come to understand these principles more thoroughly for ourselves.

Home schooling can also broaden the teacher's horizons. Being born and raised in Canada, Elizabeth was taught the British view of the American Revolution, and she never really heard much about the American Civil War. We studied the Civil War in home school last year, and Elizabeth had the opportunity to revel in the rich tales of that part of American history—its pain and suffering, the heroes and heroines who made big differences, and the Underground Railroad. This expanded her understanding of the different attitudes prevailing in the South and the North. And now that we are studying the American Revolution, she is getting a solid look at the other side of the story.

Some people fear that their children won't learn the right things. This is what published curricula are for, and there are "scope of study" books available to show you what the average public school student is supposed to know.

Some people fear that they are not good teachers. Many of us don't feel that we are teachers at all. But if we are parents, we are teachers, whether we like it or not. (The bumper sticker on our van reads, "Every home is a school—what do you teach?") We all teach by example, and often the best example for a teacher to demonstrate is a willingness to learn and an interest in (not necessarily a passion for) the subject. Our children are going to forget much of what they learn. Will they remember that Texas is the leading producer of beef cattle in the United States? Does that really matter? We don't believe so. What we do feel matters is that our child is learning how to think and how to research a subject. She will probably forget that fact about Texas, but we are doing our best to make sure that if she ever needs to know that fact, she will know how to find it for herself. That is the difference between teaching a child *what* to think and teaching *how* to think.

I am not interested in all the topics my child must study, and I have been told that the good teachers are the ones who love the subject. There is some truth in that, but we believe that what makes a teacher effective is a love directed at a different subject—the child. You don't have to know the different properties of the elements. You don't have to remember the five steps of the scientific process. That's what the curriculum is for.

Can I really do a better job than a professional teacher who has gone to college to learn the best ways of teaching children? There are two prerequisites for effectively teaching a child: to *know* the child and to *love* the child. Fortunately, this is a straightforward task for any parent who chooses to make the commitment.

Teachers in classrooms with twenty pupils have a hard time really getting to know their students. Excellent teachers manage to do the job, but it can take many months to know each student. Is it possible for a teacher to love a child in the classroom in the same way that the child's parents love her? The love factor can make a tremendous difference.

We know our children's limits. We know when they can be pushed to go a little further. We know what level of work they are capable of, and it helps to know what's going on in other areas of their lives. We know if they were up late the night before, or are ill, or are overexcited about a coming event, and we can make allowances for that. As their parents, we have great insight into what sparks their interest, what their weaknesses are, and how to motivate them.

According to Ray Ballman's book *The How and Why of Home Schooling*, the average public school student receives about six hours of individual attention from the teacher each year. That comes to about two minutes a day! Any parent can beat that record.

Will I be consistent? Probably not all the time, but no teacher except the Lord is perfectly consistent. There will be days you would prefer not having to teach, but your children (and you) will benefit from the discipline of doing something because you made the commitment to do it, not because you feel like it.

You *can* teach your child, and with very few exceptions, regardless of your limitations—physical, emotional or relational. When you are called by God to do something, it may not be easy, but it is *always* possible. Your limitations (whether a lack of patience or a lack of mobility) will make it harder for you, but home schooling is a whole-family activity, and Mom and Dad are an essential part of that family. They also need to learn.

Do you find it hard to concentrate on teaching something as elementary as vowel sounds? God may be helping you discover and develop a new strength. Do you have a personality conflict with one of your children? Perhaps that is the child who should be in school while you work with the others at home. Or perhaps God wants to redeem your relationship as you teach the difficult one at home.

Parents Who Are Not Qualified
Are there parents who aren't qualified to home school?

There probably are.

A local public school official reported receiving a phone call from a woman who wanted to home school her kids. The woman was barely articulate, displayed wretched grammar and constantly interrupted the call to scream threats and obscenities at her kids over the TV blaring in the background. Not a pretty picture.

Parents who cannot read, write, do simple arithmetic or control the household probably should not home school, at least not as a solo effort. (A co-op schooling situation could provide an environment where parents can learn alongside their children.)

Parents who are not motivated to give their children the best possible education available should probably not home school. Laziness is not a good reason to keep the children at home.

A parent who is not willing to set aside a career to sufficiently deal with educating a child should reconsider. Usually it's the mom who has to do this. If she feels resentment about staying home, it might damage her relationships with her child and husband.

Remember that certification is not normally the issue. Courage and determination, mixed with loving insight and commitment, are the distinguishing features of the *qualified* teacher.

9

Is Your
Family
Ready to
Home School?

Some families desire to home school but face
circumstances that present serious obstacles. Home schooling
can be difficult for single parents to do, but some succeed. One
single parent who home schools describes her situation this way.

> I am a single parent of three. I wanted my children to be home
> schooled, but couldn't figure a way to do it until I talked with my
> eldest daughter, now twenty-four. The only employment she could
> find in our area was a minimum-wage waitress job; instead, she
> agreed to teach my two younger daughters (twelve and fourteen)
> in exchange for room and board. That made sense to me, both
> emotionally and financially. I make enough money to support us
> all, and we are all pleased with the situation.

A rural businessman lost his wife suddenly and faced the task of
continuing the education of his home-schooling family. He realized that his children were old enough to teach themselves from

the curriculum books and that the oldest were quite capable of keeping their small farmstead going while he was in town.

Single parents may also be able to work at home (telecommuting or running a cottage industry) and home school children at the same time. It's harder, but it's not impossible.

The Family with a Special-Needs Child

Is yours a "special-needs" family? Does your child require special attention for a physical, emotional or mental disability? Do you have a highly allergic young child who needs constant supervision in regard to diet and activities?

Our daughter's asthma and allergies were a factor in our decision to home school. At the age of five, she was not always able to tell when she was starting to have difficulty with her breathing, and she could not always identify the foods most likely to have milk products (her trigger) in them. She was very susceptible to cold germs and seemed to pick up whatever was going around. She had a lot of trouble with asthma during her colds, and we knew that kindergarten is a fabulous breeding place for cold germs and viruses. She was not able to administer her own medicine, and school rules did not allow her to carry her medicine with her. By the time she could sense her condition, tell a teacher and get to the nurse, she might be well into a painful, dangerous and even fatal asthma attack.

Our daughter now is old enough to monitor her own symptoms, and we are grateful that we did not have to concern ourselves with alerting different teachers and staff to her potentially dangerous condition.

Missionary Families

Is your family on a foreign mission field? Home schooling has proven to be a successful way of educating children who are living in a foreign culture. Sometimes a missionary's children can fit into the local school system, but often the school system has very different teaching methods, as well as completely different requirements. This can be a complication when the child is ready to transfer credits and academic records to a school or college in her native country.

We tried a local preschool for our two eldest in the African city where we were missionaries. Our socially adept eldest did well, but the second child was unhappy. We were unable to afford the local private schools, and the public schools were not even an option to us. We chose to home school—the only practical option open to us and other local missionary families—and it worked well. We shared materials among families and did group activities together. Whenever we returned to the States on furlough, we bought as many good books as possible, saving them up for the day the various kids would be ready for them.

The Blended Family

Is your family blending two or more cultures? How important is it to you that your children understand all of the cultures that have contributed to your family? The public schools are doing much better at it in recent years; however, it is still difficult to teach children in any depth about a foreign country or a minority culture. (At least the schools have gotten away from uniformly Caucasian depictions of all children in their books and materials. But there is a lot more to culture than the color of people's skin, hair and eyes.) If you or your child are native to a culture that is vastly different from the one you are living in, consider how your schooling choice could supplement that learning.

Is Your Family Able to Home School?

Are your personalities compatible? We have observed that successful, happy home schoolers generally do not show signs of stress. Possibly they felt some anxiety when they started, but they didn't by the time they got to the finish line.

Is home schooling compatible with the ministries to which you have been called? Has God called you into an area of service that would make it difficult to home school effectively? For example, a full-time pastor and his wife might feel overextended if they had to devote a great deal more time to their little ones, although many pastors' families are home schooling.

Is the family unit willing to make changes to accommodate a new lifestyle? Changes will be necessary. They may not be great initially (especially if you start on day one with your child in kindergarten), but they will show up over time. Over the years your household, your schedule, your lifestyle and your approach to learning in general will look increasingly different from those of your friends who have their children in traditional schools. Can you live with this?

What we really believe about God is demonstrated more clearly by our actions than by our words. Home schooling works when we realize that our pupils are our partners in learning; we must be ready to explore and grow alongside our children.

10

Are Your Children Ready for Home Schooling?

You may be ready for home schooling, but are your children? As you try to identify the schooling option that is best for your family, remember to take your children's personal characteristics into consideration. Do they tend to be passive? Independent? Rebellious? Their personalities need to be weighed before you come to a final decision.

Peer-Dependent Children

What sorts of personalities do they have? Peer dependent? That can be okay, but it can also have its drawbacks. Some children want to be clones of their friends in looks, possessions, activities and speech. Would you like to break that dependency? Are your children able to entertain themselves alone in their own rooms? Would you like to develop this skill in them?

I changed a lot when I had to be home schooled. I tend to act the

*way the people around me are acting. I reflect my environment.
Now I more easily reflect the godly atmosphere of my home. I like
myself better now.* (twelve-year-old)

Are you concerned about how easily your children succumb to
peer pressure? Do they tend to be joiners, following the behavior
of other children regardless of how negative it is, simply because
it is what others are doing?

*Structure is something I have to create for myself now. I wish I
was more organized. School used to do the organizing for me.*
(fourteen-year-old)

Children can see some of their own shortcomings:

*I know I picked up bad habits when I attended public school—
laziness, disrespect for parents and school authorities. I guess I
was easily influenced by the other kids, and I wanted to fit in.
Since home schooling, I've had to work at changing those habits
and attitudes.* (fifteen-year-old)

Independent Children

Or are your children fiercely independent in their thinking and
adequately self-entertaining? Our daughter is like this. It makes
home schooling easier, but she would also be fine in a classroom
setting. A cooperative preschool teacher observed this in her at
age four, pointing out that it was a little unusual to see such a
young child so unconcerned about what everyone else was doing
or wearing. She would be off in one corner doing what she chose
to do. If another child joined her, she was delighted. But if she
had to play alone, she could do so. It was more important to her
to explore her interests than to be with others.

She also was quite unconcerned about what people thought
of her wardrobe. If she liked it, she wore it, regardless of others'
stares or comments. Elizabeth had made her a full-skirted dress
with a crinoline for square dancing. When she attended a special

Christmas play, she wanted to wear that dress because she said it made her "feel nice." Despite the cold winter afternoon, she wore it, oblivious to people's stares as she "floated" up and down the grand staircase at intermission. She was in her own little world; we were pleased to see that she was not particularly vulnerable to the smirks of her peers.

What are your child's interests? Does the school situation allow the time necessary for exploration of special talents?

Once there was a little girl whose passion was figure skating. But her school schedule left her very little time to spend on the rink. Her parents switched her to home schooling; now she can finish her schoolwork in the mornings and spend two hours practicing in the afternoon before her coach even sees her. Home schooling is giving that family the opportunity to develop one of their daughter's talents without depriving them of their family time together at and after the dinner hour.

The hardest part of home schooling for me was that I couldn't participate in the school sports program anymore. I later joined a home schoolers basketball team, and that was pretty neat. I missed my school friends, but when I returned to school a few years later, I found they'd all really changed. Maybe I had really done the changing, but it was easy to make new friends. (seventeen-year-old)

Some parents come to realize that they are already teaching their children at home, and this realization clinches the decision for them to home school.

I spent almost every evening helping my kids figure out their school assignments. I finally pulled them out of school to teach them myself. It doesn't take as much extra time as I thought. Why not teach them right the first time and save the aggravation?

What sorts of experiences have your children had in the school environment? Are they happy there? A local teenager answered our survey:

I liked being in school; it taught me about working in a group and about competing with others. I know some home-schooled kids who really shy away from any kind of competition. I think this can be avoided if families that home school make sure their children are in co-op teaching situations, and participate in sports. (fifteen-year-old)

Rebellious Children

How about the rebellious child—the one who is always at odds with school authorities, family and especially parents? Home schooling may be impossible, or it may be exactly what the child wants and desperately needs. Misbehavior is frequently the child's way of begging for attention—*any* kind of attention, even negative.

A church family's middle boy was expelled from public school after a series of scrapes. Unable to afford a private school, his mother began to home school him, even though she feared their personalities and past history of friction would be an explosive combination. To her surprise, she found that the concentrated attention from her was exactly what he needed and longed for. Feeling left out as a middle child, he needed the reassurance that he was worthwhile as an individual and special to his parents.

We frequently and unreservedly refer people to Ross Campbell's *How to Really Love Your Child.* We find it to be the best single book on filling a child's deepest needs. Children long for and thrive on direct eye contact, appropriate affection, focused attention and loving discipline. This book has helped equip us for the task of rearing our children with love and acceptance. But I do know a few parents whose children seem to defy the norm, and the advice from even this special volume was seemingly ineffective for them. Handling a child who constantly defies every authority figure and rule in their life can be exhausting.

Our son challenges everything. Schooling him at home wore me out, and dealing with him made me feel that I was shortchanging my other child. It was costing us our mother-son relationship. He would purposely botch a paper I assigned him to write. I would tear it up and ask him to do it over. With several confrontations like that punctuating every day, I found that I couldn't suddenly switch roles and be the loving mother to whom he would bring his problems. As far as he was concerned, I was one of his problems. His personality type is the kind that if he can't see any direct benefit from doing the work, he can't be bothered. And he'd rather go down in flames than give in. We sent him to a private school.

Individual Learning Styles

Are your children "cerebral" or "hands-on" learners? Perhaps they have been misidentified as special-needs children. We know of several children who were labeled ADD (attention deficit disorder), and their parents were baffled and concerned. The children were active, healthy and curious, but they had a hard time sitting in one place doing desk work for more than twenty minutes at a stretch. The label had been attached to them by teachers whose primary concern was maintaining law and order.

Our family doctor just laughs when he talks about our constantly vibrating preschool children. He suggested that we home school them because he didn't think they'd survive a standard school environment. Or vice versa.

If the regular classroom cannot accommodate your children, maybe it's the classroom that needs changing, not your children. Who says that a six-year-old must sit still for twenty minutes at a time? Some children simply can't do that!

Our boy always squirmed and wiggled through his math flash cards. He did them well, but the ordeal hardly seemed worth the effort. Then I had the bright idea of throwing the cards on the floor,

*one at a time, and asking him to "fetch" them. He scrambled on
the floor after them, and when he delivered them to me, he had to
deliver the answer as well. So for now we play "math pickup."
When he's older and can sit still for longer periods, we'll do
numbers a little more traditionally.*

Children learn differently. Those who are cerebral sit still and
happily absorb the lesson that is presented to them. Some learn
better in an environment where they can bounce their ideas back
and forth with the teacher. And the active, hands-on child has to
be moving and experimenting and learning his own way; the
typical classroom is not for him.

Do your children have actual learning disabilities—dyslexia
or any other condition that frustrates learning? Home schooling
might be the only suitable environment for working around their
limitations.

*My eldest child is moderately autistic. I didn't feel good about any
of the public school options for him, and recognized that I was the
one who knew him the best. I wanted him to be in a low-pressure,
loving environment and frankly couldn't afford the special schools.
I already had the right environment for him—at home.*

*I am plugged in to some of the support systems for parents with
autistic children and feel quite confident we're doing the best for
him right now. Of course I wonder about him as an adult, but I
take great hope in the fact that many autistic children do most of
their developing in their teenage years.*

There are some warning signs that you might need to remove
your child from her present school situation. Are you seeing
academic burnout in a fourth-grader because she is being pushed
to achieve higher and higher goals? The child may need to be
placed in an environment where she has the opportunity to
perform advanced work but is not pressured into it.

Parents are to protect their children, as God our Father protects us. This is not the place for a theological discussion on the fatherhood of God, but it is a topic that always leaves me feeling safe. Our children learn about God through the way their parents deal with them, and they need to know that their parents will rescue them if need be. They may need to be removed from tough situations at school. Or they may need to be left in a tough situation to learn how to work it out.

We placed our child in a private school because we felt we could no longer deal with schooling him at home. He is a confrontational child who always seems to be getting into something with somebody. He needs a safe place. We are trying to make home that refuge for him. When we schooled him at home, then home was also the place he was having most of his confrontations.

Children need to know that they do not have to face their situation at school alone, and indeed that they will be rescued from it if necessary.

Our twelve-year-old daughter in the local public school never had any homework because she was able to complete it all during class time. She got A's in every subject. She had her own group of nice friends, but we noticed that our outgoing, friendly daughter was becoming withdrawn and sad. She was acting as though she was under a great deal of stress. She had mentioned some incidents at school that involved guns, and her personal safety was discussed, but there was more to it. She did not feel challenged in her schoolwork, and when she was assigned to work with a group of students on a project, she felt frustrated when the other students let her do most of the work and then collected good marks on her efforts.

Through this discussion we came to see the immense disparity between the philosophy being taught at school and the philosophy we taught at home. We realized that every day our daughter was being confronted with an ideology that was a complete 180-degree turn from our own. She needed some decompression time every day after school to readjust to our home environment, and it was obvious this was the cause of her unhealthy silence.

We prayed about it. We considered home schooling, but I didn't feel prepared to jump into it in the middle of the school year. After making several phone calls, and after tightening our budget a bit, we decided to put her in a nearby private church school. We held our breath waiting to see what would happen in the winter-spring semester. To our great delight, we saw her challenged in ways that she had never before encountered in a school. She was ready for it, and had to work harder at her studies than ever before. When she got an A, she knew she had worked for it and was really proud. But more importantly, our family feels that we are not exposing our children to ideas and attitudes that cannot reflect God.

Children want to learn. How those things are presented, and with what materials, can make a world of difference to how well they learn and how much they enjoy it.

11

How Do You Know Where to Start?

Curriculum selection presents a particular challenge to those who are getting started in home schooling. Many questions arise.

"How do I know what curriculum is most appropriate for my child?"

"Will I be able to teach the difficult subjects that it includes?"

"It's expensive, and I'm afraid I'll end up buying something that isn't going to work."

"Can I return it if I don't like it?"

"Can I get help in using it?"

"What happens if my children decide they don't like it, and teaching with it becomes torture?"

In order to select an appropriate curriculum, you must first know your child. Cathy Duffy's book *Christian Home Educator's Curriculum Manual* helps you assess your child's style of learning and leads you to types of curriculum that will be most workable for you. Don't start home schooling without reading it or Mary Pride's *Big Book of Home Learning.*

Second, don't buy curriculum material until you have physically examined it. Home-schooling associations conduct annual one- or two-day conventions that feature speakers and workshop leaders, for a reasonable fee. Among the many exhibitors at these conventions you can find anything that relates to home schooling (and a few things that don't). A convention is a good place to look through the books you and your child will be using, and publishing representatives are right there to answer your questions. In fact, you need to keep asking questions until you have answers that satisfy you. Some curriculum publishers may offer you a great deal—for example, no shipping costs—but don't feel pressured to buy anything you aren't sure you want.

Some parents spend an entire day of the convention in the exhibit hall, which gives them an opportunity to discuss the materials in greater depth. Sometimes you can purchase just a pass to the exhibit hall and thus avoid paying for workshops you don't attend.

If you are not able to examine the materials you order ahead of time, you can usually return materials you don't use. When you place the order, check to see what restrictions exist on the return of the materials. Some providers will allow you up to ninety days to return unused curricula. Shipping costs can be high, but it's better to pay for extra shipping than for a curriculum you won't use.

Third, look at what your friends are using. Ask them your questions. Many home schoolers begin with a curriculum that a friend is using because they like knowing that if they need help or direction, they have it right there. Sometimes you can borrow a used curriculum for a while to see if you and your child really like it. If you don't know any home schoolers, contact your state association. It can help you find someone nearby with whom you can talk. Most home schoolers are friendly and approachable. They are willing to listen, and they like to share their ideas. After all, that's how most of us got started—with lots of help from others.

I purchased a beginner's reading curriculum years ago for $14. I used it with my child and passed it on to a friend. She used it for her two and has loaned it out to at least four other families. Talk about a great investment! That $14, along with our time, has started at least eight children on their way to great literature.

If all else fails, and you end up with materials you cannot or do not use, you can try to sell them. (But be aware that some publishers do not allow you to resell their books because you are purchasing the right to use their material to teach one child, not buying the material itself.) Many support groups have second-hand curriculum sales every year; if the one closest to you doesn't, you can start one. All you need to do this is a church basement, tables and some advertising. (One local group we know used the seating area of a roller-skating rink while their children skated!) Recycling! It's a great way to get rid of what you don't need, help others get what they need, and recoup at least part of your initial investment. Secondhand bookstores might take the materials, or try your local shoppers' newspaper—often called something like *Trader, Swapper Shopper* or *Thrifty Nickel.* We have purchased materials through our local *Trader.*

What if it turns out that your children do not like the curriculum you select? Perhaps you can make little changes that will please them. If you like the material but the children don't, perhaps it is just their way of saying they don't want to do school at home. Were they excited about the idea of home schooling, or did they just go along with it? It could be that no matter what curriculum you choose, they won't like it.

My son resisted the first reading curriculum I chose. I couldn't figure it out. It was fun and easy, with great pictures. He just resisted it, no matter how I presented it to him. So I gave up and tried something else, but not with much better success. A year later, when he finally did learn to read, he told me that he hadn't wanted to learn to read because he thought that I wouldn't read to him anymore.

Perhaps you realize midstream that this material you have chosen isn't for you. It will be up to you to decide if you should see the year out with that curriculum, or if you should change immediately. If you have chosen a mainline curriculum and you don't have any philosophical problems with it, try slowing down or speeding up. For example, Bob Jones math is good for children who need review and reinforcement in math principles. It doesn't push the child too quickly and returns to the same ideas over and over. And it's fun. However, if your child is a whiz at math and doesn't need a lot of review, then A Beka may be the way to go. It moves a little faster. Keep an open mind about it. If you have just purchased the entire A Beka curriculum and find that the math is too fast for your child, perhaps you should consider changing the math to Bob Jones. If your child is interested in math concepts and loves the ideas behind the exercises, try Cornerstone.

Fourth, don't select a curriculum too far ahead. Your child's rate of development and personal interests can change quickly. Some families prefer to use the same curriculum for all their children. It's easy to keep track of, some books can be reused, and Mom gets to know the material very well. But be prepared for the possibility that the curriculum you use for an older child won't fit the next in line. (Better to sell it, in that case, and start fresh with a program more suited to the child.)

There are no recipe books for home schooling, but the two mentioned at the beginning of this chapter come pretty close. If you had to learn to cook without a cookbook, you would learn by watching others, knowing your ingredients and trying a few simple things first. Once you mastered those, you would try something else. Then you would borrow recipes your friends had come up with and would try them out yourself. Although your friend's family loved her concoction, your family may not. Flexibility and a willingness to change—your ideas, yourself, and maybe your curriculum—are essential. Very few home schoolers at the end of their career are using the same curriculum they started with.

Fifth, for your first year, select a standard program, perhaps along the lines of A Beka, Bob Jones or Calvert. They can help keep you on track, especially in the higher grades.

For parents who are starting home schooling from the very beginning, I suggest that you go slowly. Ease yourself into it alongside your child. You may not even need a curriculum as such. A few little workbooks along with your own ideas (depending on your child's interests and abilities) will suffice for kindergarten. It might be helpful for you to visit a kindergarten and observe exactly what the children are doing. Chances are you have already done much of it with your child, and you will see that what goes on most of the time is creative teaching in a fun, play-filled environment.

We started by reading Mary Pride's *Big Book of Home Learning* series and were overwhelmed at the cost of the curricula. Sticker shock, I called it! We examined as many of these materials as possible at our local state convention to see what was being covered and realized that for kindergarten, and even first grade, we could do it ourselves with a few different materials. We chose math by Bob Jones and *The Writing Road to Reading* for first grade, along with KONOS. That was ample for us. By the end of second grade we had extended our language arts to include *Learning Language Arts Through Literature*. Between those programs and the support group we were involved in, both of our children were getting a thorough education in everything mentioned in any scope and sequence book. We also used computer games and activities. When we were finally able to afford a CD-ROM, a whole new world opened for the children's exploration. Then there were the books the children absorbed—some of their own choice and some of the ones we planned for us to read.

But it is not necessary to spend a lot to get good materials. Consider carefully what subjects really need to be covered with a formal curriculum (see a scope and sequence book to help you decide what subjects must be covered and what areas your child already has proficiency in). In the early grades it's basically the three Rs. An excellent resource to help you see how basic this can be is Ruth Beechick's books *The Three Rs* (three brief books for K-3). They are very reasonably priced and are well worth reading and rereading. You can use her ideas yourself without investing in a curriculum, depending on what your child is capable of doing. Cover the basics (reading, writing and arithmetic) thoroughly at the beginning, and your child will be able to jump into virtually any curriculum a little later on.

Children love brightly illustrated workbooks. When our daughter was doing first grade and using a few colorful workbooks, our son (then age four) wanted something to do too. So we spent about $10 on preschool books that helped him form letters and numbers (the wipe-off pages are great) and added a few items to our collection of Cuisinaire rods, pattern blocks and puzzles. He had his own little box of school supplies and used them whenever he wanted to do school with us but couldn't be included directly in what we were doing. As he grew, we bought some of the supplemental workbooks for children by Golden Books, and the Basic Skill Series. These can be found at teachers' supply stores and even at some of the big drugstore chains.

Consider your needs as the teaching parent. Some curricula come with one teacher's manual that covers all the subjects. Others have a different teacher's guide for each subject, and if you multiply that by two or three children, it can get hectic!

I went crazy trying to keep track of all the different teacher's guides for the curriculum we used to use (I'm teaching four). I liked the material, but I guess I just wasn't organized enough to do it that way. So we've switched to a system that has one teacher's guide for each grade level. What a relief!

Some curricula require you to make a lot of preparations. Do you have the time for this? Are you at the library two days a week anyway? Do you like to participate in the planning process, or are you a parent who wants all materials to be placed at your fingertips?

I love KONOS. It really gets me involved in what my children are doing. I can control which activities we do and even make up my own. It takes a fair bit of time, but I find that in the preparations I make, I'm really preparing myself to teach the material. It's lots of fun.

Do you want materials that are specifically based on the Bible? Some include a spiritual application in many of the lessons. If that is not what you are looking for, there are many materials that are just solid academics, neither ignoring nor emphasizing the Bible.

I didn't really want materials that are always referring to the Bible. I just wanted solid material that would teach my child what he needed to know. I liked the way many curricula were set up, but frankly, the ever-present spiritual message was not what we wanted. So we chose something secular.

Most families find that what they choose works fine. But as they continue home schooling, their needs change or they realize that another product is better for them. So they switch the next year.

You name it, we've probably tried it. It's a little embarrassing to admit that, but when I remind myself that it was necessary to do so, I realize that I'm a better teaching parent because of it. We had a couple of moves in there, and different children in different schools when we started. I started with two of them the first year of home schooling and soon saw that one needed something different. Then the littlest one needed something age appropriate, and a couple of times our choice really didn't work. Once we did finish the school year with it, and the other time we changed in the middle of the year.

The more you read, the more you equip yourself to identify what will work for you. It's okay to change something that isn't working. Every curriculum you use will assist you in selecting another.

The "piecing" method—some of this and some of that—has worked for us because I was able to grow with my children in terms of time commitment, more detailed work, and a wider variety of subjects to be covered. But now that the children are older and I am busier, we have decided to use Calvert, in spite of the cost. It didn't take us long to realize that the cost of Calvert, even with using the advisory teaching service, was just a fraction of what it would cost to put our child in a private school.

An excellent program for teaching your child to blend sounds and begin reading is *Teach Your Child to Read in 100 Easy Lessons.* Everything you need to have and say is written out in the book. You don't need flash cards, manipulatives, cassette tapes or videos. All you have to do is snuggle with your child for fifteen to twenty minutes every day and work through the lesson to-gether. It's fun, it's easy and it works for most children. (The stories and pictures are probably too juvenile for most eight-year-olds.)

One mother we know decided to prepare her own curriculum. We admired her ingenuity and hard work. She kept things pretty simple. Her boys were young, and she started with the three Rs. She used the library and referred to materials she borrowed from friends. A lot of parents may not feel confident enough to do this themselves, but there are many inexpensive supplies for those who feel the money crunch.

Keep it simple! It's easy to overwhelm young children with your own enthusiasm for "doing school." Foster in them a delight of learning and discovering things on their own (with your guidance). Go with their interests. What lights up his eyes? What does she talk about for hours? Those are the books to look for in the library. Those are the activities and field trips to arrange.

Our best studies were initiated by one of the children. We'd get books on those topics, and we'd all be looking for related materials. Make school something that your family can participate in together, and something that fits your lifestyle and convictions, even if it turns out to be quite different from what your home-schooling friends might be doing.

We invested in some good paint pots (the kind that hold the brush in with a matching top), lots of brushes, a dry-erase easel and stand (and pens), large sheets of art paper, construction paper, scissors, stamps and stickers, crayons, chalk, paint and so on and made a lot of play dough. (See recipe in back of book.) These were the basic supplies in every preschool and kindergarten classroom we saw.

We have used a variety of curricula—the do-it-yourself stuff and the prepackaged, everything-in-a-box approach. We find that the prepackaged format is a lot more conducive to our particular lifestyle and needs right now. Planning for this kind of curriculum basically involves reading ahead in the teacher's manual to make sure we have the necessary materials available and to see what we'll be covering in the next week or so.

The material our daughter covers has become a lot more structured. This is good for her. She has specific material to cover in a given day to stay on schedule. Occasionally she even gets ahead a bit, but I make sure she is never behind. When we were piecing our curriculum, it was easy to let little bits of it slide, rationalizing that we would get to it another day. (We didn't!) I wanted her to do more, to be able to push herself a little further, and I wasn't sure I was going to be able to do that without the backing of another authority—the school curriculum and the advisory teacher.

Parents who are removing their children from school to teach them at home would certainly benefit from using a complete curriculum past grade one. Do the research, choose one and use it for the year. After that you will have a better idea of what does and does not work for your child. Few home-schooling families use the same curriculum throughout their children's educational career. It's okay to change your mind. But if you stick with a mainline program, your child will be taught basically the same sorts of things each year. If you remove your child from a private school, perhaps you can continue with the same materials. Many Christian schools use the same curricula that are available to home schoolers. This would ease the transition, since you are already familiar with the work.

Educational Entertainment

Some of your curriculum work has been done for you. And it will be showing soon on a TV or computer screen near you. Not all TV is mindless and corrupting; not all computer games are violent, gory and pointless; not all magazines are shallow and choked with materialistic advertising.

Our public TV station has provided many shows that entertained our children while teaching them at the same time. *Sesame Street* and *Mr. Rogers' Neighborhood* were the first to draw their attention and loyalty. Then we found *Reading Rainbow, Shining Time Station, Magic School Bus, Bill Nye the Science Guy, Where in the World Is Carmen Sandiego?* and *Kratt's Creatures. Wishbone* has rekindled their interest in classic literature. *Nova* and *National Geographic* have fascinating specials on topics from Stonehenge to deep sea life to space exploration. There are many good videos (specifically Christian or not) that can be rented, borrowed or purchased.

The computer has captured our kids' attention as well. *Snoopy's Yearn to Learn, Dangerous Creatures, Ecoquest: Search for Cetus* and the *King's Quest* series have absorbed them for hours, expanding their thinking skills and their understanding of the world.

Magazines also fall into this category. Our children have enjoyed and benefited from the *Babybug, Ladybug, Spider* and *Cricket* magazines, as well as *Kids Discover, National Geographic World,* and *Highlights for Children.*

The best curriculum is the world around us. We keep our eyes open and remind our children frequently that school is always in session.

12

Are You
Really on
Your Own?

Home schooling may seem to be a lonely business that keeps you shut up alone with your kids, with no help in sight.

But the truth is much more comfortable than that. You have more resources available to you than you may realize, both before and during the actual business of instructing the kids. The challenge comes in accessing the resources and making them work for you. Once you get going, it comes easily.

You need only turn to the resources listed in this book for the extra advice and material.

Support Groups
A support group is a local gathering of home-schooling families who meet on a regular basis (weekly or monthly) for a variety of purposes. Some groups may include forty to fifty families, while

others may consist of three or four families.

Their purpose is to encourage and support one another. Parents gather to talk about their needs, frustrations, triumphs, and to pray together. Guest speakers may occasionally address an informational meeting.

Most support-group meetings focus on the children. These range from informal play times to highly organized study times, such as a history or language club. Some of these groups are built around a common curriculum that all the families are using. They use their times together to do group projects, presentations and field trips.

Some support groups have requirements for membership. These could amount to as little as casual attendance or as much as agreeing to a dress code, signing a statement of faith and making a commitment to faithful participation. And some groups, depending on their needs, have a small membership fee to help cover basic expenses.

Our personal experience with home-school support groups has been varied. Our present one consists of four to six families with eight to thirteen children. Some teenagers are studying a different (and much more difficult) curriculum, and they do not join us regularly. We all use the same curriculum for science and social studies—one that focuses on character qualities. The moms take turns preparing and hosting the two-hour meeting.

These activities have three major benefits. First, they help keep our family's studies on schedule. We are answerable to the other families and feel motivated to keep up with the others. If that were not the case, we could easily let some of the material slide and then find ourselves not adequately covering the materials. Second, we need the contact with other families. We share materials and ideas, and the sense of support and encouragement helps us through the school year. Third, our children have the opportunity to share their academic work with other children in formal times of presentation, as well as in informal discussion and interaction.

As is the case with most support groups, the children range from infants to twelve-year-olds. The infants are there because their moms are there, and the children generally participate in at least some of the activities when they reach four or five years of age. Our children are learning to relate to others who are younger and older than themselves, to others who are better and poorer readers, to others who are more advanced physically and to little ones who are just learning to cut things out. It teaches our children tolerance and respect for people who are different.

Support groups also ease the logistics of field trips. A factory, farm, office or museum may have minimum requirements for the size of tour groups. Two or three support groups can band together to meet these minimums.

The very first support group we belonged to focused on the young child. Our older child was then eight, and we kept things simple with lots of games, seasonal activities and field trips, and straightforward, safe science experiments and crafts. Younger siblings stayed with a couple of moms in the nursery facility of the church building we used. The extent of our "organizing" was a phone list and regular planning meetings. All of us were Christians, and we felt pretty comfortable with the ways things were going.

But one day we had to decide on a statement of faith and membership requirements. We received inquiries from a family that belonged to a popular sect, and we realized that we had to establish our formal purpose. Although we were not interested in reenacting Sunday school every week, we did want to teach our children in the light of God's Word, viewing everything from a biblical perspective. We realized that a home-school support group could be a wonderful vehicle for witnessing to others and decided that we did not feel comfortable before the Lord excluding people because of their beliefs. But still we did not want our children exposed to heresy. So we compiled a statement of faith that is very straightforward and basic. It included a purpose statement and asked all members to refrain from teaching their beliefs unless they concurred with our statement of faith. That particular family decided not to join us, but soon a non-Christian family joined us who traveled quite a distance to our group. The one that was closer to them resembled a Sunday school, and they felt uncomfortable with it. This mother and her children joined in on all our activities, and I like to think that we all did a little planting in their hearts.

Another non-Christian mother joined our group after visiting for observation, mainly because her autistic son was accepted without comment—and even with affection and consideration—by both the adults and the children. "You really do care about *all* the kids, don't you?" she remarked to us after her first visit.

Some support groups assume that the moms will team-teach. For example, let's say that four families commit to supporting each other. After each family has finished with reading, writing and arithmetic in the morning, one mom takes all the children on Monday afternoon and teaches science for an hour and a half. On Tuesday another mom takes all the children and does art and music. On Wednesday it is history, and on Thursday geography and social studies. On Friday, everyone gets a nap! This arrangement allows every mom to have two hours off three afternoons a week.

And don't look past other people you know well. Relatives, neighbors and friends who have specialized interests and expertise would probably be pleased to come and talk about their interests, show their collections or demonstrate how such and

----

such works. Many retirees are delighted to be given an opportunity to have children ask them about their particular interests. Grandparents are a wonderful resource, and many of them enjoy being called on for their particular expertise.

One year we participated in a history club. Our state historical society has a junior division, and for a very minimal fee we were added to their mailing list and had access to activities for children in fourth grade and up. We met every other week, and Dan's father, a lifelong history enthusiast and unqualified supporter of his grandchildren, became the club teacher (our two children plus three children from another home-schooling family in the neighborhood). Meanwhile, Mom had a lovely break. They each had a copy of A Beka's *My State Notebook,* and they enjoyed filling in bits of fascinating information about their home state. Every time we went somewhere of interest, we took the camera so we could get a photo of our members standing in front of a historical marker or a museum. They built many memories as they filled their notebooks, and years from now they will be able to look back on our experiences with fond memories.

Names and phone numbers for local support groups should be available from your local home-school representative, but there are casual groups that aren't known officially, and the only way you'll find out about them is by asking around and keeping your ears open. The group that suits your family best may be located across the city, so don't limit your search to your immediate neighborhood.

Most support groups are open to visitors. Visiting various groups is a good test of how your children interact with other members. Some parents begin to visit groups a year or two before their children even begin schooling, just to get to know other people and perhaps to start building solid relationships. Larger groups often have some preschool activities, as well as nursery facilities.

If you are unable to find a support group that suits you, start your own. Start small and simple and keep it easy to handle. As your group grows and becomes established you can expand and enhance. This will begin to happen fairly naturally as your children get older. Sometimes a play group is all you need for the early grades—a time to be with other home schoolers, to swap ideas, to encourage and commiserate, and a place to let the children play and build friendships. After that you may decide to arrange a few field trips and special activities, and grow from there. You can use your own home, or you can check out churches in your area. One of our support groups found a church that let us use its facilities—gym, classrooms, nursery and preschool rooms—free. We were grateful for their generosity and gave them a small gift of the money left over from our membership fees at the end of each year.

A caution about support groups: be sure you understand what is expected of you. One family was involved in a biweekly group. It was always on their calendar, and they never missed without a compelling reason. But other families in the group did not share their sense of commitment and often "just didn't get there." Nor did they call first. Our faithful friends became disillusioned and switched to another group where commitment and consideration levels were more evenly matched.

Another kind of support group is the co-op teaching group. It functions like a regular school, except that you meet only one or two days a week. The children are separated by ages or grade level and take a certain class for a semester. This is a neat way to teach trigonometry. Younger children may be studying something like American geography or literature; first- and second-graders may be working on science or language. Preschoolers are in a preschool environment, and babies are in the nursery. Several families share the jobs, and they usually spend the entire day together. They may switch to different classes during the day and may have lunch together.

A co-op learning group requires a great deal of organization and commitment, but if you have the manpower, it can work out nicely. Churches are usually open to providing a suitable facility, either free or for a small fee.

Local Resources

Libraries are plentiful, and our experience with librarians has been very positive. Home schoolers are no longer a novelty, and many of the branch libraries in our area have a special book section set aside for them. Many librarians know the home schoolers in their neighborhood, and they can be very helpful. If you go during the day when public school kids are in the classroom, you can meet and befriend other home schoolers. They're easy to spot!

Many libraries offer opportunities for children to gather for reading times, movies or special seasonal activities. Libraries usually have small meeting rooms, and, depending on your age and space requirements, may be willing to let you use their facilities.

Buy annual museum passes so you can visit frequently, or find out which ones are free or have free days. An excellent children's museum in our town has sponsored classes on everything from pollution to sharks, dinosaur digs to a planetarium. These classes can make exciting supplemental material. All of this is in addition to their permanent displays, which the children love to visit over and over (especially the hands-on science center).

Check into your local zoo. Many offer intriguing classes and opportunities to help care for the animals.

Take advantage of groups like Girl Guides and Boy Scouts, 4-H clubs, and your local YMCA. Keeping track of these opportunities means reviewing your local papers regularly.

Bigger churches offer extra activities open to children: choirs, plays, sports, clubs and so on. Church membership is not always required, so look beyond the church you are attending.

Do you have a computer, or have you been thinking about acquiring one? If so, you are in for wonderful treat, since there is a growing supply of excellent software programs that really challenge your child to think out options and plan ahead.

Any time your child spends on the computer is an opportunity to simply learn about computers. The possibilities with a computer are limited only by your imagination and your pocketbook. If you already have one, you probably know what we mean. Ask other home-schooling families which programs have been most useful to them. You may even be able to borrow some for a while to try them out yourself. And your local computer bulletin boards will frequently have programs that may prove to be quite useful.

The *Magic School Bus* computer programs are probably the best home-schooling purchase we have made. Both kids have spent long sessions at the keyboard exploring the solar system, the human body, the ocean and the interior of the earth. Computers require active involvement—they do not just entertain. The computer is ready whenever they are, and neither parent is required to supervise; the computer will gladly play the same activity over and over and over and *over* again without impatience or fatigue. And the kids are learning! The *Magic School Bus* has taught the kids more about those four subjects already than we knew before we went to college.

State/Provincial Organizations

Every U.S. state has an association of home schoolers, as do most Canadian provinces. There is a smattering of them in other countries. In the United States these groups lobby for legislation,

----

educate the public and provide services for both new and established home schoolers. Most of them conduct annual home-
schooling conventions. If your area does not have a convention,
it might be benefit you to find the one closest to you and plan to
attend.

Books and Publications

There are several good home-schooling magazines to choose
from. (Names, addresses and subscription information are listed
in the resources section of this book.) They offer a wealth of fun
ideas, listings of resources, art and craft projects, science experiments and math ideas, reading helps, field trip information, news
of interest to home schoolers and so on. They also contain
encouraging and insightful letters from other home schoolers.
But be sure to use these items as sources, not measuring sticks!

*One of the home-schooling magazines features a family in each
issue. Most of their stories are interesting, and frequently give good
ideas. But when we were first home schooling, I found, after
reading one of these articles, it was easy to feel disorganized,
incompetent and ineffective as a teacher. Of course, I was measuring myself against these other families, and that was unfair for
me to do. Most of these families had been home schooling for many
years. I was just a beginner. And most of these families had
something unique about them, or at least something of special
interest, and we are just an ordinary, everyday family with a dad,
a mom and two children. We couldn't write an article about
ourselves for a magazine like that. I was foolish to allow it to
make me feel inferior. I was in fact, comparing my weaknesses to
their strengths.*

"Of making many books there is no end" (Eccles 12:12). A few
helpful ones are listed in the resource section. Most are for
teachers, but some are for students.

13

How Much Will This Cost?

Home schooling does not have to cost much at all. After looking at catalogs and talking with home schooling friends, we realized that the costs were well within our budget, no more than what it would cost to outfit our children for the local public school.

We used secondhand materials where we could, and we visited the library frequently. (Home schoolers are good about selling their used materials at discounted rates.)

We have done many interesting projects with common household items. Elementary science and art can be done in the kitchen, the sewing room or the workshop.

We already had a fair amount of scientific, technical and computer equipment on hand. Dan fixes electronic gadgets and has a workshop in the basement. We already had a home computer, and he is adept at finding low-cost software the kids can use and enjoy as they learn.

What about the income that is lost because Mom is out of the marketplace? Must you have two incomes to provide for the needs (not wants) of your family? Although you want to home school, are you afraid that you cannot get by on one salary? Serious budget planning and prayer may be in order. Write down everything (yes, all of it!) you spend for a three-month period. Identify everything that you would not need to purchase if one parent were at home and the children were not in school.

Christian Financial Concepts, Inc. (see resources section of this book) is one excellent resource for advice on restructuring and simplifying your financial affairs. You may be in for some surprises. We were surprised to find that Elizabeth would have to earn about $40,000 for us to realize any financial benefit from her employment. The additional income would place us in a higher tax bracket, our second car would always have to be in good condition, Mom's wardrobe would need a major upgrade, and there would be tuition and child-care expenses to plan for. We would probably hire someone to clean the house for us at least twice a month, we would eat out more often, and we would have to pay someone else for the many tasks that Mom does. She would not be able to take the same amount of time to shop as carefully as she does. And how do you put a price tag on the added stress that our family would experience?

But what are the nonmonetary costs of home schooling? There are some, and they can be thought of as the drawbacks of home schooling, depending on your viewpoint. You may have to give up some of your freedoms (or perceived freedoms) and make changes in your lifestyle and home.

Home Schooling Is a Lifestyle
If you are seriously considering home schooling, your home is

probably a learning center already. That does not mean that you have expensive equipment for science experiments or the latest computer for each child. It means that you are willing to accommodate the latest project and let your home decor share space with some unusual articles.

One guest in our home commented on the tall set of shelves in the kitchen corner that overflowed with paper, crayon boxes, felt-tip markers, colored pencils, magnets, chalk, play dough, glue, miscellaneous art supplies and equipment. He said that seeing it made him wonder if we were home schoolers.

Not every family with such a shelf home schools, but you would be hard pressed to find a home-schooling family that does not have something like it. A supply shelf can be an eyesore, but few of us can afford the lovely storage systems featured in home decorating magazines. We simply have to adopt an accepting attitude toward such aspects of home schooling.

We have only one wall in our pre-World War I home that is large enough to accommodate our history time line. (This is a chart that we fill in with little stick-on figures as we study that time or character in history.) It is in our dining room on the one wall that faces our living room. That space would be perfect for some lovely piece of art, and I (Elizabeth) was not excited about putting the time line there. I was hoping that we could be a little more discreet with this collection of bits and pieces of paper! But up it went, and I gradually became used to it. It is becoming more and more cluttered as we add things to it. But the children love it, and I appreciate the sense of linear history it displays. It is not a piece of art in the classic sense of the term, but many guests comment on that time line. People note that we are a home-schooling family because we have it on the wall. And some people (especially history buffs) examine it closely. Taking it down one day will mean the end of a very special era.

The house takes a beating because it is both a residence and a school. Our home is bright and comfortable, but it is not a show-place. It shelters four human lives under constant construction. Some home-schooling families set aside one room as their school-room. They have desks and charts and all their school equipment in there. We heard of a family that built an addition to their home for this purpose. But we don't have that option at the moment, so we use what we have—the kitchen table, the dining-room table (and floor), the family room and, whenever possible, the outdoors.

What are the essentials? A table and chairs, a storage area for supplies like paper, pencils, art equipment and so on, a specific place for each child to keep school things, and some kind of file for storing samples of their work and school records. We use shelves, and each child has several for texts, notebooks and things like flash cards and review sheets. We find that office stackers serve this purpose well.

I'm a neatnik. I thoroughly enjoy having a place to put everything, and then doing so. I find it difficult to function in a cluttered environment. Friends compliment me on my clean house, but they don't always realize that my neatness is more evidence of my shortcomings than of my strengths. Some people are capable of functioning wherever they are plopped down, and they do a great job. I get uptight about messes, and I am continuing to learn that sometimes the Lord is not going to grant me the luxury of a totally neat environment. A Bible verse jumped off the page at me recently: "Where no oxen are, the crib is clean: but much increase is by the strength of the ox" (Prov 14:4 KJV).

The caption "A clean desk is the sign of a sick mind" has always bothered me. Guess why? But there is an element of truth there. Where work is happening, there is going to be stuff lying around, at least while the work is taking place. I don't mind it as long as I'm in the middle of it, and believe me, I've been in the middle of some royal messes as we have worked on our house and have completed book projects! But my level of tolerance decreases in direct proportion to my level of involvement or interest, and the Lord has challenged me to be more tolerant of other people's messes. If the manger is clean, it's because the oxen are gone, and if the oxen are gone, so is the benefit of having an ox. I don't imagine oxen are particularly tidy creatures. If you have one, the feed from the manger will be spread all over the floor, and there will also be some other things to be cleaned up.

As a home-schooling parent, part of my strength is my children and their creative juices, their energy and imagination. To have everything in perfect order would make it impossible for them to live, learn and grow in the way God established for them. However, I do heartily endorse teaching them to clean up after themselves and to help others do so.

Home schooling can compromise parents' personal comfort:

There have been several times in my life in the process of making a major decision that I realize I do not feel comfortable about it. In praying over the issue I express this to the Lord and ask for help not to shy away from something out of fear. One day, as I was applying the "but I really don't feel comfortable with this situation" yardstick, I realized that the Lord was trying to get my attention. He was whispering in my ear, and the words I heard did not comfort me! He said, "Did it ever occur to you that I'm not all that interested in your personal comfort?" That challenged me in that particular situation, and encouraged me too. I realized that I didn't have to feel comfortable. I did need to know that what I was doing honored the Lord and that I was not aware of any reason (other than my own shortcomings) to not follow through. Freedom means following the Lord without self-centered worries. God will bless anything that is in line with divine principles.

We have been changed and we have reshaped ourselves. Home

schooling reveals your shortcomings very clearly. It exposes your character and challenges you spiritually. It is not at all a smooth, comfortable ride. But the Lord does not call his disciples to smooth, comfortable rides; sometimes he draws us outside our comfort zone to teach us something.

Our activities almost always include the children, whether we want them to or not. The only "drawback" to home schooling that we have discovered after six years is being at home every morning of the school year with our children. Elizabeth is not free to attend the women's Bible study on Tuesday mornings or have lunch with a friend. Other activities are arranged around home schooling, not vice versa.

The primary teaching parent bears the brunt of these time demands. One new home-schooling mom pointed out that she did not know when she was going to do her Christmas shopping. Her husband often worked late and was quite involved in their church. It was a real challenge for her to come up with the time to shop without her little "assistants."

Another mom mentioned that she finds it difficult to accommodate the other things that go on in her life. If one of her friends needs some help, school time can suffer. She takes in some work to do at home, and that further reduces the time she has for her friendships.

Some moms worry that withdrawing from the work force will leave them unemployable in ten years' time. That may very well be, but if you are convinced that you need to home school, you can trust God to take care of your future employment. The world is changing too fast for us to be able to predict what things will be like a decade, or even a year, from now. We need to trust the Lord for the future, not fret about it now.

Electronic Helpers
A TV and VCR are useful home-schooling tools, even if they are

not connected to an outside antenna or cable. Our children were not aware of the existence of TV programs other than videos, news, sports and a few selected public broadcasting shows until they learned to read. Our approach to TV viewing proved to bear fruit; to this day the children would generally rather read than watch TV in idle moments.

A computer is worthwhile, but not mandatory. All of our experience has been with IBM compatibles (personal computers, or PCs), and we recommend the following configuration as a minimally adequate system:

486DX2/66 processor
8 megabytes of RAM
850-megabyte hard drive
1.44-megabyte floppy disk drive
SVGA monitor (0.39 or smaller dot pitch; 0.28 is preferable)
mouse
Windows 3.11 or Windows 95
printer

A 28.8k baud (or faster) modem is required to access the Internet or on-line services such as CompuServe or America Online. A CD-ROM drive and a sound card are necessary, since many office packages, games, encyclopedias and educational titles come on CD-ROM only and feature integrated sound and narration.

A Macintosh user recommends the following minimum package:

Performa, Quadra or PowerPC (System 7 compatible)
8 megabytes of RAM
840-megabyte hard drive
printer
CD-ROM
28.8k baud modem

Remember that any computer will be obsolete soon after you buy it (or possibly before; if it's on the shelf now, there's something bigger, faster and cheaper on the truck that arrives next week). We do not send first-time computer purchasers to the popular computer superstores, as you can easily pay more than you can afford for more computer than you need. We refer people to the smaller computer shops that are found in almost every town; the proprietors can build you exactly what you need (for your budget and your requirements) and will hold your hand through the frustrations of learning how to use it.

The Positive Side of the Price

The price we have paid for home schooling has been worth the family unity we have developed, a way of life that honors the value system we espouse, and the spiritual and moral development of our children.

The kids are in or around the house all the time. We know where they are, and we don't have to look far for signs of life. We share their day and aren't left wondering what they did all day in school. We can apply the things they learned in their schoolwork to a pertinent life situation. Our son was learning about pronouns, for example, and I (Elizabeth) had explained to him that you must use a noun first, then refer to the person, place or thing with a pronoun. Without the noun, the listener couldn't know what was being referred to. Later the same day he caught himself starting a new topic of conversation with "They were . . . " and corrected himself with a big smile. I knew why he made the correction and was proud of him for remembering and making the application on his own.

Our stress levels are minimal. We arrange our daily schedule according to our physical limitations and Dad's job requirements, and we have remarkably few illnesses (the result of being exposed to fewer germs?). Every day we must face our fears about meeting our children's educational needs, and this keeps us on our knees in prayer.

We are together a great deal. If we get caught up in busyness, at least it's a joint effort. Getting formal school out of the way in the mornings gives us more hours in the day for extracurricular events and outings. (How many families actually sit down to eat even one meal together every day?) The kids have accompanied Dad to the junkyards, computer shops and bookstores; they have helped pull the lever in the voting booth; they have helped pick and carry groceries and care for various pets. They participate alongside us in "life its own self."

Our children are happy, and we delight in them. We like the persons they are turning out to be, although we won't see the final result for years.

We chose this option partly because we liked the way we saw home-schooled kids interacting with others. They were friendly (to people of all ages), polite and considerate, not easily swayed by the latest fads and fashions. They seemed secure in their understanding of who they were and who God wanted them to be. They liked being with their families, and most of them were committed Christians. It was also quite obvious to us that they were well advanced in their schoolwork.

Home schooling has not cost our marriage anything. In fact, we would say that the opposite is true. The flexibility we experience in our school year and daily timetable is a plus for us as a couple. We are not subject to the sometimes demanding requirements of the local school's activities. We have more time to be a family, and when our family is together, we are together as a couple. Our marriage benefits from the times we take a day off to visit a state park to let the children explore the woods and collect specimens for a science report.

Finally, there is no way to reckon the value of having Mom or

Dad available to nurse a little one through an illness. And how do you measure the value of having the time to curl up with your children to read? Or teaching them to cook favorite meals? Or having the time to take a walk to collect stones for a building project they have going on in the backyard?

Every decision in life has a cost associated with it. There is a cost to doing and a cost to not doing. Some prices will be paid gladly, others reluctantly. The point is to seek the greatest benefits for the most reasonable costs.

14

How Can You Make This Work?

How practical is home schooling? How can you reorder your life to accommodate this adventure? We tend to break the focus into three or four main areas.

You must be committed to your children as they are with an eye for what they can become. We cannot prevent our children from being exposed to sin by home-schooling them. We are both very accomplished sinners, and our children take after us. In fact, they tend to have the same character flaws we have. As we struggle with controlling the problems in ourselves, our children observe us and find out what does and does not work. They see our frustrations. They see our failings. They are asked to forgive us. And we all learn together. No environment is going to be perfect. But some environments are better than others, and one or two are probably far superior to the rest.

As I have had to learn to overcome certain weaknesses and sins

*in my life, I am now better equipped to help my children do the
same because they carry much of me and my bent to sinning in
their hearts and minds.*

Our children are a work in progress, as we are.

We lighten our load through the school year by doing some
schoolwork through the summer, when the heat and humidity
send us indoors. This allows us to maintain the level of compe-
tency we achieved at the end of the previous school year. So we
don't need to spend the first few weeks of the new school year
trying to get back to where we were at the end of May. This is
particularly important for little ones, as they tend to forget their
phonics and math without regular review.

Squeezing in about fifteen days of school during the summer
months means that we can take off every other Friday during the
regular school year and have a few days left over for special treats,
activities or sick days. We don't count the days the children are
sick. They do a full year's work, even if they are sick four times.
We always make it up. That doesn't happen when you send your
child off to school. Our children's playmates seem to miss a week
or two of school each year due to illness.

You must be committed to home schooling. But it's a funny kind
of temporary yet wholehearted commitment. You have to be
diligent and self-disciplined. You can't get away with doing
school when you "feel like it." (Besides, that attitude is not setting
a good example for little ones.)

It is necessary to set long-term goals, to evaluate and reevalu-
ate your progress and to steer yourselves back onto your original
course.

You must believe fully in what you are doing because you will
be questioned regularly about your decision to home school,
often by people who want to challenge you rather than encourage
you. If you live in an area where the public authorities actively

discourage home schooling, you will need a strong conviction of the Lord's calling in order to withstand the hassles that will probably come your way.

Yet you maintain the freedom to *not* home school in the future. Your commitment is serious, but not necessarily forever.

When we announced that we were planning on home schooling our five-year-old daughter, one of the questions we were asked was, "What are you going to do about teaching her calculus?" We hadn't even gotten that far in our own minds, and certainly weren't prepared to explain it to anyone. We said that we planned to take one year at a time. The question was intended to show us that we had not considered all the implications of home schooling, and at that time we felt a little defensive about our choice. We tried not get derailed by that sort of question, but we have remembered it, and every so often we pull it out to reexamine it.

We still have no firm idea how we are going to handle calculus. Will Dad teach her? A tutor? Can she teach herself through a book, video, or interactive computer program? We aren't sure, but we aren't worried either. We have learned enough of God's ways to know that if teaching our daughter calculus at home is what God wants us to do, we will find a way to do it.

It's okay to say, "We aren't sure this is working anymore, and we would like to try something else." It does not mean you have failed. The Lord directs us through changes in our lives, and what works for children when they are six or seven may not be what works when they are twelve or thirteen.

Circumstances have changed. I quit my job to further my education, and my wife now has to work. So we have placed our son in an excellent Christian school. We are happy with his progress and his character development, and we know that this is what the Lord wants for us right now. We home schooled him until he was in sixth grade. By that point he was getting restless. Since he has no siblings, we felt that going to school was a good opportunity for him. The Lord timed it all perfectly.

Some parents commit themselves to a two- or three-year plan and evaluate their progress at the end of it. Then they start fresh with the decision-making process. They may decide to continue home schooling. They may decide to try the local public school or a private school.

More advanced subjects can be taught through a co-op teaching situation. There are a wide variety of curricula that focus on math and science.

You don't have to set up your school like the school you remember. Your child doesn't have to sit still and quiet in your home! Learning can be active and fun.

You must be organized and flexible. There are many helps available to get you organized, keep your records straight and help you plan your school year. But no calendar, time planner or schedule is of any help if you do not follow it, and that is where discipline comes in.

Some of us are naturally disciplined and find it very difficult to function without a schedule or in an unstructured environment. There are people who love making lists. They function better when they can glance at a piece of paper and see what still has to be done today. They take great delight in crossing something off the to-do list. But it can become a security blanket. Then they have to work at actually letting something on the list get put aside for a wonderful opportunity that arises out of the blue. No list can be allowed to take precedence over what is the best for the family. The Lord has used home schooling to teach people to be more laid-back, to relax and let God plan the day and the school year.

We have a big calendar by the kitchen phone that tells all.

Everything gets written down there. Every appointment, library book and birthday is recorded there. If we lost that calendar, we would be sunk. There is also a calendar that shows the week at a glance. It is prepared on the weekend for the following week. We transfer information from our big calendar to that sheet of paper and fill in the names of people we need to call, which day we do the groceries (and the grocery list grows on the back), and other little household chores that don't get recorded on the big calendar. That list stays by the phone. I (Elizabeth) scribble down phone messages on the back, and anyone who moves it better have a *very* good reason.

Several home-schooling parents, both those who started with kindergarten and those who started later, have admitted that home schooling is easier on both the child and the parent if the child had never attended school.

A twelve-year-old told us:

I'm not a very organized student. When I was in public school, the teachers sort of did that for me. Now that I'm home schooled, I have to do it myself—keep myself on the schedule we've worked out, and finish my work in reasonable time. It's kind of a drag, but I guess it's really good for me.

The child with little experience in a classroom environment is likely to feel less challenged by doing things differently, and the parent grows into the "school every day" lifestyle gradually. There is a big difference between the stress experienced by a mom who starts to teach her five-year-old at home with a kindergarten curriculum and schedule, and that experienced by a mom who takes two or three of her children out of school simultaneously and starts them in different grades with full-day schedules.

We grew into schooling at home. When our daughter was three, I attended a co-op preschool with her. This was a good experience for both of us, but the September after her fifth birthday, we started home school. Since we were already doing a lot of what was suggested in the scope and sequence books for kindergarten, it took only forty-five minutes a day to cover our kindergarten material. A little bit of reading, a little bit of writing, and a little bit of arithmetic was sufficient.

Sometimes I would spread these activities out over a couple of hours and insert art and music, and on some days we met with a support group or had field trips. The actual teaching time was low-key and (mostly) low stress. We gradually increased the amount of time and the variety of subjects covered over the next two years. By second grade we were spending two or three hours each morning doing math, phonics, writing, reading, Bible and either art, science experiments, history stories or geography as time permitted. It's easy to spend the entire morning doing school with the children. We don't even think about doing otherwise.

Other families have tried public schools first:

We withdrew our eldest child from school midyear and the other two the following autumn. It was a real adjustment, and I wished that we had been able to start from the very beginning of their schooling.

Jumping directly into teaching your older child at home in later years is going to be harder, but many parents do it. Just be prepared for some stress, and remember that whatever led you to withdraw your child from school was probably causing even more stress. If you are able to begin home schooling at the start of a school year or grade level, it will be a little easier to find an initial pace that suits you. Most curricula are designed to start with a review of basic concepts and introductions to topics, so the going is usually fairly simple and straightforward. Some parents choose to start by doing three or four days the first couple of weeks and then gradually pick up the pace if they can. If you need to, take a week off to catch your breath.

Don't expect to be able to jump into teaching three children three different curricula. As a matter of fact, that would be a good method for burning yourself out. There are curricula that enable you to teach children of different levels from the same materials. These are generally unit studies, and KONOS is an excellent one. All of the children would be studying the same topic (for example, bridges), but the older ones would prepare drawings of suspension bridges and conduct research on different suspension bridges while your little ones would build bridges out of blocks or Legos. This is an effective family teaching strategy, and it is really fun. Your next vacation may very well include a discussion of the bridge you just drove over: is it a cantilever bridge or a beam bridge?

Flexibility within the organization is critically important. Although we get the sense that Jesus was a busy man, we never have that feeling that he was hurried. He was always ready to change plans or slow things down.

Targets of Opportunity

We feel that it is good for the children to see us being entrepreneurs and continuing our own studies as adults. This helps reinforce the idea that learning and growing never end.

One day seven-year-old Jennifer announced that she was going to make books, just like Daddy. She went to her room and began to create a few books. One was about cows, another about whales and so on. Then she declared that she was going to sell them. We asked her how she planned to do that, and she promptly informed us that she was going to set up a table in front of the house and sell them there. We exchanged secret smiles, knowing she was headed for disappointment. We live on a quiet street, and no one is shopping for something created by a seven-year-old artist-illustrator. But we gave her permission to pursue her idea.

About forty-five minutes later Elizabeth went out to see how things were going. Jennifer smiled up at her mother and informed her that she had sold three already. Another potential customer had gone home for a quarter. (One customer was a guest of a neighbor who had parked on our street. She was so taken by our little girl and her creativity that she bought two!) Elizabeth was astounded but tried not to let her amazement show. We both just shook our heads in amazement. Jennifer continued to create and sell books off and on over the next few weeks and was able to add a few dollars to her piggy bank. She had gotten the idea from her father, but she had developed the marketing technique herself. We were delighted with her entrepreneurial skills and applauded her efforts. (And we were among her customers. The book is tucked away in a "memory box" along with the children's first hair clippings and baby teeth.)

Then there was the *Titanic*.

Robert Ballard discovered the *Titanic* in 1986. Jennifer discovered the *Titanic* in 1991. Anything to do with that ghost ship caught her immediate and undivided attention. She watched the video, wore the pages out of her collected books and drew endless pictures of the departure and disaster. To this day, when she draws a picture of a ship it's likely to be black and red with four funnels—one of which, she will proudly tell you, is hollow and is used for baggage only.

Her interest helped direct one family vacation toward Boston and the East Coast. We visited two *Titanic* museums and wandered around Woods Hole in search of Robert Ballard. One of the first historical dates she learned was 1912, and we could tie family (and later world) history to that year. "Your grandfather was born nine years after the *Titanic* sank. Your great-grandfather was born eighteen years before the *Titanic*." We wondered at times if we could simply reletter the calendar to B.T. and A.T. The

Titanic was Jennifer's initial key to integrated learning. Home schooling gave us the opportunity to indulge her fascination any time of the day or year, whether or not "school" was in session.

An opportunity with Andrew is referred to in family lore as "A Visit from Skippy the Prairie Dog." The morning alarm went off, and a bright-eyed bundle of boy jumped into our bed and burrowed under the covers. Safely hidden, he emitted some very strange woofing sounds. "Are you all right?" Dan asked, peering under the blanket.

"I'm Skippy the prairie dog!" came the answer. "I'm barking!"

"Do they really bark like dogs? Are they mammals?"

"I think so," came the muffled reply.

"I don't think so," said Dan. "I think they're rodents."

"Rodents?"

"Squirrels. Mice. Chipmunks. Rats. They're all rodents."

"Oh. Okay, I'm a rodent!" He came out long enough to give Dan a kiss and then disappeared back into his burrow.

Later that day, at the library, we checked out books on prairie dogs, which Andrew promptly read or listened to. He learned more about rodents than he expected, and he loved every minute!

We have taken great delight in the occasions (and they are not at all rare!) where something shows up that is exactly what we need for a subject we are currently studying. It may be a magazine article, a TV special, a book, a guest in our home or a stray animal that needs help. Though we live in a city and have a very small yard, we have (so far) provided temporary care for nineteen chickens, two tadpoles/frogs, a turtle, several birds, countless insects, a wandering dog and eleven bunnies—all coexisting with our permanent cat collection. Most of these guests were unexpected but fit in beautifully with what we were studying. We have to be ready to flex the schedule to fit around these serendipities. (And be ready to recognize them as well; some of these opportunities looked more like burdens and interruptions at first.)

Time Compression

A home-schooling parent with two or three children needs only half the time to accomplish work that a teacher in a classroom with twenty pupils needs. The parent (usually Mom) knows her children well, knows what level of work to expect from them and understands when to push a little harder and when to back off. A teacher can focus on only a few students at a time, usually the ones who are getting bored or getting lost.

The parent at home does not have to occupy one child with busywork while the others catch up. That child can go on to something new or finish leftover chores.

A junior-high teacher whose wife home schools their five children told his pupils at school that his children were finished with their schoolwork by noon. They all groaned but soon realized how that could be when they considered what they actually did with their entire school day.

Some couples are able to arrange their work schedules in a way that allows them to school their children at home. If Dad works regular daytime hours and Mom works a part-time job at night, she can probably manage to juggle the hours of schooling. But what about the stress to the marriage? This is part of the cost of home schooling for a family like this, and realistically, it is a price many couples are not willing to pay.

I am a nurse and work three twelve-hour shifts a week—two days on the weekend and then one other day during the week. On that day I can leave the children with a relative, and Dad has them on the weekend. I realize that as they grow and require more time for school I will probably have to drop that extra day of working during the week. Of course, we hardly ever get to do anything as a family, and it is putting pressure on our marriage. We are hoping that this will not have to last much longer.

Usually a part-time job works out better for Mom than a full-time job. It can be beneficial by getting her away from her pupils and giving her some time with other adults. Older children can take more responsibility for their schoolwork and do not require a parent to be with them. Some families with teenagers just give them the assignments, which they do on their own.

Some couples are able to share a job. They have the equivalent of one income, and they both participate in the education of their children. Some moms are able to share a job with other moms, and they swap child care and home teaching. It sounds pretty challenging, but it can be done. Of course, if there is the possibility of working from the home, this could simplify juggling work and home schooling.

As children get into higher grades, the focus should shift from a mom-to-child relationship to a student-to-material relationship. Mom may very well still be there to guide, but the student becomes responsible for almost every aspect of the work. Many families like to use a correspondence high-school course because this gets the student accustomed to a relationship with a teacher apart from Mom and Dad, with deadlines to meet. One such curriculum uses videos for lectures. Some community colleges allow high-school students to attend classes. They may not actually be able to get credit for the class, but they will get excellent exposure to the subject material and the classroom environment.

Lecturing is a time-honored method of teaching that is respected because it simplifies the way one person (a professor) can deliver information to many people (the students) at one time. It is not the only teaching technique. Sometimes it is an excellent technique, and many of us have had delightful teachers and classes that were structured around this style of teaching.

However, many of us have also suffered and endured classes simply for the credit. Depending on the subject and the teacher, it may or may not be effective. If you feel that your teenage student must attend lectures, video courses may be well worth looking into.

This is where co-op teaching helps fill gaps for high schoolers. I attend a co-op class twice a week for algebra, chemistry and philosophy. I find myself measuring my work against what the other students are doing, and sometimes it gets a little competitive. But it's really neat, and I'm glad I can do it.

To get more information on what is available in your area along these lines, contact your state association of home schoolers.

One group we know of offers classes in biology, physics and chemistry for two weeks in June each year. It is open to home-schooled students aged twelve and older. It is taught by teachers who have just begun their school break, and they meet every weekday morning for two hours of fairly intensive lab work.

How to Home School

We could write many more pages on ways and means that we and others have found useful, but that is not the purpose of this book. The many volumes listed in the resources section offer good guidance and wise counsel toward making a home school work well for all involved. Use them frequently, intelligently and well.

15

How Can You Decide?

What do you do with all this information?

Make a chart, as we did.

When we reached this point in our own deliberations, we compared public school to home school. The other options at that point were not feasible for us or desirable in our eyes.

We ruled out private schools (both secular and Christian) on the grounds of cost and accessibility; we couldn't easily afford them and didn't want to spend our adult lives in the van zipping back and forth across the city.

Boarding school received no consideration from us because we had our children to *have* our children, not to give them over to the care of strangers.

We thought about parochial school at some length. The nearest one has a good academic reputation but would have cost us more than we felt we could afford. This school also is becoming known as a destination for kids who make trouble in public school and need to be taken in hand. That doesn't contribute to a great learning environment for the other children, so we crossed that one off the list.

We discussed the possibility of moving into a different school district or moving closer to some of the schools that we had considered. But the expense that would be involved was prohibitive for us, and besides, we liked where we were, as well as its proximity to Dan's work.

We had to know what the potentially negative consequences of each choice might be, since our children would have to live with them.

When our daughter was starting first grade, a casual acquaintance asked Elizabeth what the bad part of home schooling was. We were a little taken aback at first, partly because no one had ever put it in quite those terms and partly because we thought there wasn't any. Elizabeth paused until she realized that she was not free to be involved in anything during the day at our church—women's Bible study and prayer time—or to have lunch dates with friends.

Try the following. List all the schooling options you are currently considering. Write them on separate pieces of paper as illustrated on the chart on pages 121-23. Make two columns under each option, and label them "pro" and "con." Then start filling them in. Write out what you see as the good and the bad consequences of each option. It may take you several days or even weeks to compile a fairly complete list. Examine your list for each option carefully, and then compare it with the others. Which consequences would you prefer that your child deal with? Which set of drawbacks would you choose for your child? Which set can you not live with? Are you really sure that the consequences will be as negative as you think? For each option, ask some families who chose it to describe their experiences. The possible negative consequences of any choice you make can last for many years, possibly the rest of your child's life.

What you list in the pro column will be the perks, as it were. Are they worth the negative consequences? Are you sure that they really are as good as you think they will be?

We have included the list that we made and continue to add to as we and our circumstances change and grow. We expanded it to cover a variety of possible scenarios. This process helped reinforce for us that we are doing the right thing for our family at this point in time.

Some items on our chart may be irrelevant to you. Make your lists personal. They are supposed to help *you*. Feel free to adapt this one to help you start your own.

	Home-Schooling Pros and Cons	
	Pro	Con
S O C I A L	Our family is together, learning to work alongside each other on a daily basis. We are building lifelong relationships with each other. We have greater opportunity to influence our children morally.	As a teaching parent, I am with my children *all* the time. I am unable to get away from home on my own during the day for shopping, social contacts and so on. I have to take the children with me or arrange for child care.
F R I E N D S	Our children experience minimal peer pressure, and we can control how much and from whom. We have more control over who our children's friends are.	Our family has to work hard at planning time with friends. Our family needs to be careful not to become overprotective and not to limit our children's friends only to Christian friends.
S C H E D U L E	We have lots of flexibility for vacation, weather, work schedule, doctor's appointments and health considerations.	We must discipline ourselves to stay on schedule. To use our time wisely requires planning and preparation (this depends on the age of the child and on the curriculum).

S P E C I A L N E E D S	This is a great option for children with special needs—physically and mentally challenged, hyperactive, gifted, emotionally disturbed, physical or emotional immaturity and shyness. The curriculum can be tailored to each child's level and rate of progress.	Am I handling any behavioral problems appropriately? Am I adequately equipped to meet the unique needs of my children? Will I shield my children too completely from the world?
C O S T	We exercise complete control over the cost of the curriculum and extracurricular activities.	We pay taxes to the local school system without receiving any direct benefits.
L E A R N I N G	Academic lessons can be applied in everyday situations, and we know exactly what our children are learning. Our children observe that learning happens all the time and is not limited to any classroom.	Our children do not have many opportunities to learn to work in a group in a room full of other children, who may be a distraction. Most schoolteachers have specific training in certain classes (especially in higher grades) that might be helpful to our children.
T I M E	Our child finishes academic instruction in two to four hours and has lots of time for extracurricular activities and other lessons.	
G R O U P S	We control what groups our child participates in.	Our child does not learn to share a teacher with twenty other students. Our child does not learn to work in a large group.
P E E R S	Our children are not isolated by age. Age segregation does occur in connection with other activities.	Sometimes our children may need a special friend of their age, and we have to work at arranging that for them. The teaching in a classroom is age appropriate.

I N V O L V E M E N T	Parental involvement is high. Parents have the opportunity to learn along with our children and thus supplement our own education.	This requires research, preparation time, reading, teaching time. Depending on the curriculum chosen, staying on top of all the child's reading and assignments can be tough.
S P I R I T U A L	As the teaching parent, I grow in my dependence on the Lord and in self-confidence.	I find myself struggling with self-doubts.

Preparing this list of pros and cons taught us a lot about ourselves. We can see that the con side reflects our shortcomings and weaknesses, as parents and as teachers. It points up our limitations and our struggles. But it also shows where we are learning, and we believe that these areas are ones where we are growing. The Lord is teaching us just as we are teaching our children. He is using home schooling to smooth out our rough edges, sharpen our thinking and mold us into more effective tools for God's kingdom. It isn't easy, but it is working.

You may still have many unanswered questions. They may be so significant that you select an option other than home schooling for your family. Every question you have asked (and managed to get a satisfactory answer for) will equip you as a parent involved in your child's academic career, no matter what option you choose. And the unanswered questions will keep you looking, listening and open to creative options in education.

We once heard a home-schooling dad say that anybody who had to really think about whether or not to home school probably should not do it. We struggled with that statement because we were thinking hard and long about home schooling and didn't see why that should disqualify us. On the contrary, it seemed to us that much thought was *required* before taking such a step.

In retrospect, we think he meant that if God was showing you that you should home school, then it was a "done deal." If you kept debating it after that, you were not really prepared to obey in spite of unanswered questions. (Part of following God means that there *will* be unanswered questions.)

The man's statement caused us to question our ability and preparedness to home school. We think we would have benefited from a book (like this one) that would have steered us through our questions and also would have challenged us with ones we had not yet considered, while encouraging us to identify our questions and clarify them in our own minds.

We did not have that opportunity. You do.

Those Who Choose Not to Home School

There are no rules about who should or should not home school, but observations and suggestions from people you respect may be helpful. After all, they know you and watch how you deal with your family and issues in your life. To home school or not to home school is a personal and highly subjective decision, and no one can decide it for you. You are the person with the answers for your family. Just as it is important to know why you choose something, it also is important to understand why you do not choose something.

We chose to home school for a year because of health reasons, and the next grade for our child was going to be taught by a teacher we had some problems with. We are enjoying the benefits of being at home (not having to be out of the house before dawn on cold mornings to clean off the car and having lots of time together), but we are lonely. I really miss the contact with other moms, and my child doesn't get to be with very many children. He wants companionship with his peers. If we can't get settled into a satisfactory support group, we may go back to school next year. I also feel a responsibility to be involved with other families so I can witness and minister to them.

So what happens if you try home schooling but feel that it just isn't working? If you are convinced that God wants you to continue, be sure to keep up contact with several other home- schooling families. They can encourage you as well as point you to different approaches and methods. When possible, include your child in decisions you make about curricula and support groups.

But if you come to the point where you are no longer sure that home schooling is what God wants, or you believe God is directing you elsewhere, it is probably time for you to do something different.

With the freedom to choose to home school or not comes the responsibility to wisely judge our personal motives for doing so or not doing so. Parents can fear the outside world so much that they continue home schooling simply to avoid contact with it. Parents may also choose home schooling because they have an intense need to exercise control over their child.

There are many valid reasons for choosing to not home school, such as:

☐ Either the husband or the wife does not fully support the idea.
☐ Both parents must work full time.
☐ A child is severely handicapped and requires specialized teaching.
☐ One parent is severely handicapped and unable to care for or provide for the children.
☐ There is a severe personality clash between the teaching parent and the child.

☐ There has been a traumatic experience in the parent's life, such as divorce, death, a change or loss of employment or a chronic or severe illness.

☐ An older child is causing serious disruption in your family, and you are spending a lot of time dealing with that problem.

☐ The main pressure to home school comes not from the parents' convictions but from (perhaps well-meaning) friends, relatives or neighbors.

☐ You believe strongly that God wants your family involved in the local school system.

Some of these situations involve temporary problems that eventually may be resolved. But when there is significant stress in the home, it's generally not a good idea to introduce yet another potential source of stress.

☐ *My son and I love each other, but our personalities pit us against each other. I know I'm supposed to let the experience of teaching him at home open me to letting the Lord teach me how to get along with him better. But I just don't feel I can do it right now. . . . There are some other pressures in our lives right now that seem to be draining me. . . . I honestly feel that if I spread myself too thin, I will snap. At least I know that at school he is being challenged academically and that he is on course. Perhaps someday in the future I can reconsider home schooling him.*

☐ *My son has a combative personality. He seems to do well in the classroom with a teacher who is a stranger. He likes to challenge everything at home.*

☐ *I couldn't home school my children because I don't have the patience, the self-discipline or the ability to do it.*

☐ *My child and I don't get along very well in tense situations. I can't imagine what it would be like to have to deal with her every day and try to get her through her schoolwork without us screaming at each other.*

Do these mothers sound like you? These comments express their perceptions of themselves in relation to their children. Their perceptions may not necessarily be accurate, but what people believe about themselves does influence their actions.

Assessing how well you handle your children at home can be difficult to do on your own. Perhaps you would find it helpful to ask a trusted friend who knows you and your family to help you answer these questions.

☐ How do you handle the discipline and training of your children? Do you feel that you have strong, loving control of them?

☐ Do your children manipulate and control you?

☐ Do you perceive a serious personality clash in your relationship with your children?

☐ Has impatience on your part ever caused problems to exist between you and your children? Do you think that this an area where the Lord is especially wanting to shape you?

Personality conflicts with your children can make it difficult to teach them. Sometimes the Lord will specifically show parents that they need to teach a child at home and work through the conflict they are experiencing, but too much exposure to each other can exacerbate the situation and make the learning environment a trying one for both of you. It might be preferable to allow the children to learn in a school and to work on the personality conflict away from a learning situation.

Some parents have children who absolutely do not get along with each other. To expect them to work effectively on their studies in the same environment would be asking too much of them. One family solved this situation by sending one to school and keeping the other at home.

A parent who is struggling with a personal issue will have a difficult time taking on the additional responsibility of teaching the children. In such a situation the children will probably do better in an environment separate from the particular problem that Mom or Dad is dealing with.

All factors considered, the decision is yours. We trust that you have fairly evaluated all sides of the relevant issues in order to make a responsible choice. If you do choose to home school, one of your first tasks will be to explain your decision to others. Keep reading.

16

What Do You Tell the Neighbors?

If you opt for home schooling, your family and friends will ask the same questions you have just worked through. Your parents will want know why your old school isn't good enough for their grandchildren. Your neighbors will want to know why the kids are home all day.

Here is a list of the ten questions that people ask most frequently, along with a few recommended answers—short summaries of some of the ideas we have covered in this book. Remember, a soft answer turns away wrath; your questioners may be challenging your decision as well as attempting to educate themselves.

Frequently Asked Questions

1. *What about socialization? How will your kids ever learn to get along in this world if they aren't regularly interacting with other children?*

Each age group has strengths and weaknesses. When twenty children are gathered together in a single room, these weaknesses and strengths are amplified and multiplied. A six-year-old can be silly without assistance. Two six-year-olds can be eight times sillier. A roomful of six-year-olds can be silly beyond belief.

Blending ages seems to produce a better environment for learning maturity and keeping order . . . and is more like the real world.

Age doesn't matter so much in the real world as it did in school. Children are shown to make friends with other children their age, and to step out of age or grade levels is quite unusual. But this does not help equip them for the real world, and I regret the many potential friendships I never tried to develop simply because the person was a little older or younger than me.

How often do you work or talk with other people who are exactly the same age as yourself? It is much more realistic to have a variety of ages, names and cities of origin in any kind of gathering. This diversity is what makes life interesting.

One of my favorite things about home schooling is that I get to be with children of all ages. When I was in school, I never had the opportunity to be friends with someone younger or older than myself.

Children learn a lot from each other when they are placed in mixed-age classes. The younger ones listen to what the older ones are learning, and they absorb amazing amounts of knowledge in a very short time. The older children can share their understanding with the little ones through games and quizzes. This activity reinforces their learning, as well as being fun. But, understandably, this is not a convenient arrangement for public school classrooms.

2. *But won't your children be different?*

A grandmother expressed this concern to her daughter-in-law, and the new home-schooling mother said, "But they already *are* different, and we want to teach them now that it is a strength, not a weakness."

Children who *aren't* different are indistinguishable from the crowd, but average people do not change the world.

3. *How do you know that your children are where they should be for their age academically? Will you recognize their weaknesses and be able to work with them in those areas?*

Home-schooled children can be tested annually and ranked against their peers in the public schools. Tutors are available for problem areas, and there are teachers' groups that for a fee will regularly check your child's progress and provide recommendations. Some curricula offer advisory teaching services that help parents assess their children's progress and development.

4. *Is home schooling against the law?*

No. Different states have different requirements for schooling, so it is important to know what your local government says about it.

5. *How do your children get the opportunity to present projects or perform in front of others?*

Support groups are an immense help. Many home-schooled children also participate in Sunday-school programs, drama clubs, music lessons and sports.

6. *Aren't children being stifled if the only major influence in their life is their parents? Don't they benefit from exposure to different styles of teaching, different teachers and different personalities?*

Home-schooled children can be exposed to many different types of teachers. The parent is the main teacher. Then there's the sports coach, the music teacher, the Sunday-school teacher and club leaders, to name just a few. Many home-schooled children belong to support groups where several parents are involved in teaching. If learning is something that is always happening, then any role model in your children's life is "teaching" them. It is the parents' responsibility to oversee who those role models are. Home schooling gives parents more control over who their children's role models are.

7. *Are you qualified to be a teacher?*

Qualified or certified? Parents who love their children, have a basic education (high school or equivalent in their own private reading and learning) and are willing to make the necessary time commitments and lifestyle changes are qualified to teach their children. (Some states do require certification. See the chart in chapter seven.) One well-educated friend surprised us when he told us he had quit school at age thirteen to go to work. The rest of his education, which was demonstrated in his lectures, preaching and counseling, was the product of his own personal reading and study.

8. *What about college? How can home-schooled children apply for college? Do they have to write SAT exams?*

A growing number of colleges accept home-schooled children. Any child can take the SAT, which most college admissions personnel consider a key indicator.

A home-schooled friend of ours who applied for admission to a college was told to obtain her GED because she had no formal diploma. She wasn't happy about it, but she took the GED test. She received the highest score in the state, winning a scholarship in the process.

9. *How will your children manage if and when you ever put them back into public school?*

The only problem that we have heard of is that home-schooled children have to learn to wait for the teacher's attention. At home, their private tutor (Mom) could get to them relatively quickly. Children who are home schooled with siblings have less difficulty with this than children who are home schooled alone.

When I decided I had reached my limits as a home schooler, I put my kids into public middle school. When I spoke to their teacher at the start of the year, she only sighed and asked, "How far ahead are they?"

10. *But home schoolers are people who have huge families and live on farms and grow their own veggies, and the women have to wear frumpy dresses and long hair . . .*

This is a false stereotype. Yes, there are home-schooling families who live on farms. But there are many more living in cities. Yes, some of us do grow our own vegetables, but that has to do with nutrition and the cost of food, as well as the joy of gardening. Some of us even bake our own bread, but so do families who choose public schools. The important thing is that each family chooses what meets their needs, not someone else's expectations. As increasing numbers of people home school, so will the variety of people who do it. We are as varied as the world's population itself.

But there is a lighter side to this lifestyle. Home schoolers give their own reasons for home schooling—some serious, some just for fun. Here are a few we especially enjoy:

12. We want our children to grow up to be politically incorrect.

11. Mom gets to play with clay and paints and people tell her she's a brave woman for doing so!

10. We can stay up late to count fireflies or watch meteor showers and sleep in the next morning.

9. We can take our vacations off-season when it's cheap.

8. Mom and Dad are forced to read all kinds of great children's books out loud to the kids.

7. The children don't have to wear shoes all the time.*

6. Some mornings are just too nice to be stuck indoors.

---

*Neither does the teacher!

5. Mom is relearning all the stuff she never really understood when she was a kid—and it makes sense this time!

4. We can buy books and build an enormous library without guilt.

3. We love the zoo (and everything else) when everyone else is at school.

2. Mom would be lonely without the children all day.

1. We REALLY enjoy being with our FAMILY!

17

Do You Need Some Final Reassurance?

We hope that reading this book has helped you clarify your home-schooling questions and concerns and has brought you closer to the path God wants you to take.

Perhaps our lack of professional educational expertise has served to encourage you. If we can make a good choice that works for our family, so can you!

We have experienced both success and failure along the way, and we have learned a lot from each. Our children are teaching us as much as we are teaching them. We are learning together, and most of the time it is delightful. However, it is important to say that if our personal circumstances and family structure had been different, our decision might have been different as well.

We may not always home school our children. The time may come when we feel that sending our children to a school would be in our family's best interests.

We have met families who home schooled for a while and then due to various circumstances chose something else for their children. But we have never met a family that absolutely regretted its choice to home school, even for just a year or two.

Whatever your decision, reading this book should have changed a few things for you. You are now better equipped to encourage home-schooling families, for you know some of their reasons and understand the conditions that come with their choice. You should be able to see how differences in personal giftings, traditions, cultures, languages and nationalities are actually strengths that God gives and uses to build up the body of Christ all over the world and to carry the gospel message to schools and neighborhoods wherever we live.

We wish you well in whatever path you choose—that all you do will honor God and advance the kingdom of God in yourselves, your little ones and the world around you.

Now to him who by the power at work within us is able to do far more abundantly than all that we ask or think, to him be glory in the church and in Christ Jesus to all generations, for ever and ever. Amen. (Eph 3:20-21 RSV)

Resources

Where Do You Turn for Help?

This is a broad (but by no means exhaustive) survey of materials and resources available for further reading or information. We do not necessarily endorse the items included in this list, but we have found many of them to be valuable sources of ideas and alternate viewpoints. Many items come highly recommended from other home schoolers and educators. All information was current as of the date of publication.

Books
Most books on home schooling and parental involvement in educating are classified 371, 372 or 649 in the Dewey decimal classification; they are classified LC37 or LC40 in the Library of Congress system.

Adams, Dan. *The Child Influencers: Restoring the Lost Art of Parenting.* Cuyohoga Falls, Ohio: Home Team Press, 1990.

Arons, Stephen. *Compelling Belief: The Culture of American Schooling.* New York: McGraw, 1982.

Ballman, Ray. *The How and Why of Home Schooling.* Wheaton, Ill.: Crossway Books, 1987.

Barker, Britt. *Letters Home.* Tonasket, Wash.: Home Education Press, 1990.

Beechick, Ruth. *The Three R's: A Home Start in Reading, a Strong Start in Language, an Early Start in Arithmetic* [for K-3]. Pollack Pines, Calif.: Arrow, 1986.

———. *You Can Teach Your Child Successfully: Grades 4-8.* Pollack Pines, Calif.: Arrow, 1988.

Bennett, William J. *The De-valuing of America: The Fight for Our Culture and Our Children.* New York: Summit Books, 1994.

Blank, Marion, et al. *The Parent's Guide to Educational Software.* Redmond, Wash.: Tempus Books of Microsoft Press, 1991.

Blumenfeld, Samuel. *Is Public Education Necessary?* Boise, Idaho: Paradigm, 1985.

Boaz, David, ed. *Liberating Schools: Education in the Inner City.* Washington, D.C.: Cato Institute, 1991.

Buehrer, Eric. *Creating a Positive Public-School Experience.* Nashville: Thomas Nelson, 1994.

Butterworth, Bill. *The Peanut Butter Family Home School.* Old Tappan, N.J.: Revell, 1987.

Campbell, Ross. *How to Really Love Your Child.* Wheaton, Ill.: Victor, 1977.

——. *How to Really Love Your Teenager.* Wheaton, Ill.: Victor, 1981.

Canape, Charlene. *The Part-Time Solution.* New York: Harper, 1990.

Chubb, John E., and Terry M. Moe. *Politics, Markets and American Schools.* Washington, D.C.: Brookings Institution, 1990.

Claggett, Doreen. *Never Too Early.* Melbourne, Fla.: Dove Christian Books, 1989.

Clune, William, and John Witte, eds. *Choice and Control in American Education.* 2 vols. Bristol, Penn.: Taylor and Francis, 1991.

Colfax, Micki, and David Colfax. *Home Schooling for Excellence.* New York: Warner, 1988.

Coons, John, and Stephen Sugarman. *Scholarships for Children.* Berkeley: Institute of Governmental Studies, University of California, 1992.

Crittenden, Brian. *Parents, the State and the Right to Educate.* Portland, Ore.: International Specialized Book Services, 1988.

Davis, Llewellyn. *Why So Many Christians Are Going Home to School.* Crossville, Tenn.: Elijah, 1991.

Duffy, Cathy. *Christian Home Educators Curriculum Manual.* 2 vols. Westminster, Calif.: Home Run Enterprises, 1995.

Farris, Michael. *Home Schooling and the Law.* Paeonian Springs, Va.: Home School Legal Defense Association, 1990.

——. *Where Do I Draw the Line?* Minneapolis: Bethany House, 1992.

Fisher, Kathy. *Homeschooler's Resource Directory 1995: The Sourcebook of Companies, Products and Services for Home Educators.* Waldport, Ore.: Brand of the Cross, 1994.

Fugate, Richard. *Will Early Education Ruin Your Child?* Tempe, Ariz.: Alpha Omega, 1990.

Fuller, Cheri. *Helping Your Child Succeed in Public School.* Colorado Springs, Colo.: Focus on the Family, 1993.

Garvey, Judy. *How to Begin Home Schooling.* Surrey, Maine: Gentle Wind

School, 1989.

Gatto, John Taylor. *Dumbing Us Down: The Hidden Curriculum of Compulsory Schooling*. Philadelphia: New Society, 1992.

———. *The Exhausted School*. New York: Smith and Varina, Odysseus Group, 1993.

Glenn, Charles. *The Myth of the Common School*. Amherst: University of Massachusetts Press, 1988.

Gorder, Cheryl. *Home Schools: An Alternative (You Do Have a Choice)*. Tempe, Ariz.: Blue Bird, 1987.

Gosman, Fred G. *Spoiled Rotten: Today's Children and How to Change Them*. New York: Villard/Random House, 1990.

Graham, Gayle. *How to Home School: A Practical Approach*. Hawthorne, Fla.: Family Learning Center, 1992.

Guterson, David. *Family Matters: Why Homeschooling Makes Sense*. New York: Harcourt Brace Jovanovich, 1992.

Hanushek, Eric, et al. *Making Schools Work: Improving Performance and Controlling Costs*. Washington, D.C.: Brookings Institution, 1994.

Harris, Gregg. *The Christian Home School*. Gresham, Ore.: Noble, 1988.

Hegener, Mark, and Helen Hegener. *Home School Reader*. Tonasket, Wash.: Home Education Press, 1988.

Henry, Carl F. H. *The Christian Mindset in a Secular Society: Promoting Evangelical Renewal and National Righteousness*. Critical Concern Book. Portland, Ore.: Multnomah Press, 1978.

Hirsh, E. D. Jr., ed. *What Your First Grader Needs to Know: Fundamentals of a Good First-Grade Education*. New York: Doubleday, 1991. (Separate volumes for grades 1-6.)

Holt, John. *How Children Fail*. New York: Merloyd Lawrence, 1964.

———. *Learning All the Time*. Reading, Mass.: Addison-Wesley, 1989.

———. *A Life Worth Living: Selected Letters of John Holt*. Columbus: Ohio State University Press, 1990.

———. *Teach Your Own: A Hopeful Path for Education*. New York: Dutton/Seymour Lawrence, 1989.

———. *The Under-achieving School*. New York: Dell, 1969.

———. *What Do I Do Monday?* New York: E. P. Dutton, 1970.

Hollingsworth, Paul, et al. *Back to Basics*. New York: Monarch, 1986.

Homeschooler Resource Directory: Sourcebook of Companies, Products, and Services for the Home Educator. Waldport, Ore.: Brand of the Cross, 1994.

House, H. Wayne, ed. *Schooling Choices*. Portland, Ore.: Multnomah Press, 1988.

Hubbs, Don. *Home Education Resource Guide: A Comprehensive Guide for the Parent-Educator.* Tempe, Ariz.: Blue Bird, 1994.

Hunt, Gladys. *Honey for a Child's Heart.* Grand Rapids, Mich.: Zondervan, 1969.

Husen, Torsten. *The School in Question: A Comparative Study of the School and Its Future in Western Society.* New York: Oxford University Press, 1979.

Hunter, Brenda. *Home by Choice: Facing the Effects of Mother's Absence.* Portland, Ore.: Multnomah Press, 1991.

Illich, Ivan. *Deschooling Society.* New York: Harper & Row, 1970.

Jones, Claudia. *Parents Are Teachers Too: Enriching Your Child's First Six Years.* Charlotte, Vt.: Williamson, 1988.

————. *More Parents Are Teachers Too: Encouraging Your 6 to 12 Year-Old.* Charlotte, Vt.: Williamson, 1990.

Jorgenson, Lloyd P. *The State and the Non-public School, 1825-1925.* Columbia: University of Missouri Press, 1987.

Kirkpatrick, David W. *Choice in Schooling: A Case for Tuition Vouchers.* Chicago: Loyola University Press, 1990.

Klicka, Christopher J. *Home Schooling in the United States: A Legal Analysis.* Paeonian Springs, Va.: Home School Legal Defense Association, updated annually.

————. *The Right Choice: The Incredible Failure of Public Education and the Rising Hope of Home Schooling.* Gresham, Ore.: Noble, 1992.

————. *The Right to Home School: A Guide to the Law on Parents' Rights in Education.* Durham, N.C.: Carolina Academic Press, 1995.

Leistico, Agnes. *I Learn Better by Teaching Myself.* Tonasket, Wash.: Home Education Press, 1990.

————. *Still Teaching Ourselves.* Tonasket, Wash.: Home Education Press, 1995.

Leman, Kevin. *Parenthood Without Hassles (Well, Almost).* Eugene, Ore.: Harvest House, 1979.

Lieberman, Myron. *Privatization and Educational Choice.* New York: St. Martin's, 1989.

————. *Public Education: An Autopsy.* Cambridge, Mass.: Harvard University Press, 1993.

Llewellyn, Grace. *Real Lives: Eleven Teenagers Who Don't Go to School.* Eugene, Ore.: Lowry House, 1993.

————. *The Teenage Liberation Handbook: How to Quit School and Get a Real Life and Education.* Eugene, Ore.: Lowry House, 1991.

Love, Robert. *How to Start Your Own School.* Ottawa, Ill.: Green Hill,

1973.

Maberry, Grace W., et al. *It's Never Too Early*. Nashville: Discipleship Resources, 1988.

Macaulay, Susan Schaffer. *For the Children's Sake*. Wheaton, Ill.: Crossway, 1984.

Mason, Charlotte. *The Original Home Schooling Series*. (Available as a set only, ISBN 188920900.) Vol. 1, *Home Education: Training and Educating Children Under Nine*. Out of print; limited quantities available through Great Christian Books. Vol. 2, *Parents and Children;* vol. 3, *School Education;* vol. 4, *Ourselves;* vol. 5, *Formation of Character;* vol. 6, *Philosophy of Education*. Elkton, Md.: Charlotte Mason Research & Supply, 1989.

McIntire, Deborah, and Robert Windham. *Home Schooling: Answers to Questions Parents Most Often Ask*. Cypress, Calif.: Creative Teaching, 1995.

Melton, James Van Horn. *Absolutism and the Eighteenth-Century Origins of Compulsory Schooling in Prussia and Austria*. New York: Cambridge University Press, 1988.

Michaelson, Johanna. *Like Lambs to the Slaughter*. Eugene, Ore.: Harvest House, 1989.

Miller, Donald E. *Story and Context*. Nashville: Abingdon, 1987.

Mitchell, Richard. *The Graves of Academe*. Boston: Little, Brown, 1981.

Moore, Raymond, and Dorothy Moore. *Better Late Than Early: A New Approach to Your Child's Education*. Pleasantville, N.Y.: Reader's Digest Press, 1986.

———. *Home Grown Kids: A Practical Handbook for Teaching Your Children at Home*. Waco, Tex.: Word, 1981.

———. *Home Style Teaching: A Handbook for Parents and Teachers*. Waco, Tex.: Word, 1984.

———. *Home-Spun Schools: Teaching Children at Home—What Parents Are Doing and How They Are Doing It*. Waco, Tex.: Word, 1982.

———. *School Can Wait*. Provo, Utah: Brigham Young University Press, 1979. (Help for the first eight years.)

Nasaw, David. *Home School Burnout*. Wheaton, Ill.: Crossway, 1988.

———. *Schooled to Order: A Social History of Public Schooling in the United States*. New York: Oxford University Press, 1981.

Pagnoni, Mario. *The Complete Home Educator: A Comprehensive Guide to Modern Home-Teaching*. New York: Larson, Burdett, 1984.

Phillips, Phil. *Dinosaurs: The Bible, Barney and Beyond*. Lancaster, Penn.: Starburst, 1995.

Pride, Mary. *All the Way Home*. Wheaton, Ill.: Crossway, 1989.

————. *Big Book of Home Learning*. Vol. 1, *Getting Started*. Wheaton, Ill.: Crossway, 1990. Vol. 2, *Preschool and Elementary*, 1991. Vol. 3, *Teens and Adults*, 1991. Vol. 4, *Afterschooling*, 1991.

————. *Schoolproof: How to Help Your Family Beat the System and Learn to Love Learning the Easy, Natural Way*. Wheaton, Ill.: Crossway, 1988.

Ray, Brian D. *Strengths of Their Own*. Salem, Ore.: National Home Education Research Institute, 1997.

Reed, Donna. *Home School Source Book*. Bridgewater, Maine: Brook Farm Books, 1994.

Reiner, Everett. *School Is Dead: Alternatives in Education*. Garden City: N.Y.: Doubleday, 1974.

Richman, Howard, and Susan Richman. *The Three R's at Home*. Kittanning, Penn.: PA Homeschoolers, 1988.

Richman, Sheldon. *Separation of School and State: How to Liberate America's Families*. Fairfax, Va.: Future of Freedom Foundation, 1994.

Rupp, Rebecca. *Good Stuff: Learning Tools for All Ages*. Tonasket, Wash.: Home Education Press, 1993.

Schimmels, Cliff. *Parents' Most-Asked Questions About Kids and Schools*. Wheaton, Ill.: Victor, 1989.

Shackelford, Luanne, and Susan White. *A Survivor's Guide to Home Schooling*. Wheaton, Ill.: Crossway, 1988.

Smith, David W. *Choosing Your Child's School*. Grand Rapids, Mich.: Zondervan, 1991.

Sowell, Thomas. *Inside American Education: The Decline, the Deception, the Dogmas*. New York: Free Press, 1993.

Spring, Joel. *The American School, 1642-1993*. New York: McGraw-Hill, 1994.

Starr. *To Learn with Love*. Miami: Summy-Birchard, 1983. Distributed by Warner Bros.

Tobias, Cynthia. *The Way They Learn*. Colorado Springs, Colo.: Focus on the Family, 1994.

Trelease, Jim. *Read-Aloud Handbook for Parents*. New York: Penguin, 1979.

Tyack, David. *The One Best System: A History of American Urban Education*. Cambridge, Mass.: Harvard University Press, 1974.

Tyack, David, Thomas James and Aaron Benavot. *Law and the Shaping of Public Education, 1785-1954*. Madison: University of Wisconsin Press, 1987.

Vail, Priscilla L. *Emotion: The On Off Switch for Learning.* Rosemont, N.J.: Modern Learning, 1981.

Wade, Theodore. *The Home School Manual: Plans, Pointers, Reasons and Resources.* Niles, Mich.: Gazelle, 1994.

Wade, Theodore, et al. *Early Years at Home: When Life Patterns Are Set.* Niles, Mich.: Gazelle, 1992.

Wallace, Nancy. *Better Than School: One Family's Declaration of Independence.* New York: Larson, 1983.

———. *Child's Work: Taking Children's Choices Seriously.* Cambridge, Mass.: Holt Associates, 1990.

Wang, Bee-Lan C., et al. *Should You Be the Working Mom?* Elgin, Ill.: David C. Cook, 1987.

West, E. G. *Education and the State.* 2nd ed. London: Institute of Economic Affairs, 1970.

White, Joe. *Orphans at Home.* Phoenix, Ariz.: Questar, 1988.

Whitehead, John W. *The Second American Revolution.* Elgin, Ill.: David C. Cook, 1982.

Whitehead, John W., and Alexis Irene Crow. *Home Education: Rights and Reasons.* Wheaton, Ill.: Crossway, 1993.

Wilkinson, Bruce. *Educational Choice: Necessary but Not Sufficient.* Brookfield, Vt.: Ashgate, 1994.

———. *The Seven Laws of the Learner: How to Teach Almost Anything to Almost Anybody.* Sisters, Ore.: Questar, 1992.

Williamson, Kerri Bennett. *Home Schooling: Answering Questions.* Springfield, Ill.: CC Thomas, 1989.

Wilson, Douglas, et al. *Classical Education and the Home School.* Moscow, Idaho: Canon Press, 1995. Write: P.O. Box 8741, Moscow, ID 83843. Tel. (800) 488-2034.

———. *Recovering the Lost Tools of Learning.* Wheaton, Ill.: Crossway, 1991.

Magazines and Newsletters

Getting your hands on just one or two issues of these magazines will open a whole world of ideas, products and curricula.

American Homeschool Association (AHA), P.O. Box 1125, Republic, WA 99166-1125. Tel. (509) 486-1351

Closing the Gap, P.O. Box 68, Henderson, MN 56044. Tel. (612) 248-3294. Computer technology for people with special needs.

Exceptional Parent, P.O. Box 3000, Dept. EP, Denville, NJ 07834-9919. Tel. (800) 562-1973

Growing Without Schooling, 2269 Massachusetts Ave., Cambridge, MA 02140. Tel. (617) 864-3100

Home Education Magazine, P.O. Box 1083, Tonasket, WA 98855. Tel. (509) 486-1351

Home Education News, Box 39009, Point Grey RPO, Vancouver, British Columbia V6R 4P1. Tel. (604) 228-1939

Home School Digest, Wisdom's Gate, P.O. Box 125, Sawyer, MI 49125 (quarterly)

Homemade Schooling, RR 1, Box 188, Atwood, IL 61913

The Homeschool ADDvisor, P.O. Box 118, Lincoln University, PA 19352 (quarterly)

Homeschooling Today, P.O. Box 1425, Melrose, FL 32666

New Attitude, 6920 S.E. Hogan, Gresham, OR 97080. Tel. (800) 225-5259

The Parents Newsletter on Special Education Law, P.O. Box 4571, Chapel Hill, NC 27515-4571

Practical Homeschooling, Home Life, P.O. Box 1250, Fenton, MO 63026. Tel. (800) 346-632; fax (314) 343-7203

Quest: The Canadian Home Educator's Digest, 12128 95A St. NW, Edmonton, Alberta T5G 1R9. Tel. (403) 293-4447

Resources: Trivium Pursuit Magazine, 139 Colorado St., Ste. 168, Muscatine, IA 52761

The Teaching Home, P.O. Box 20219, Portland, OR 97220

Under the Apple Tree, Apple Tree Press, P.O. Box 8, Woodinville, WA 98072

Curricula, Textbooks and Supplies

Duffy, Cathy. *Christian Home Educators Curriculum Manual.* 2 vols. Westminster, Calif.: Home Run Enterprises, 1995.

Pride, Mary. *Big Book of Home Learning.* Vol. 1, *Getting Started,* 1990. Vol. 2, *Preschool and Elementary;* vol. 3, *Teens and Adult;* vol. 4, *Afterschooling.* Wheaton, Ill.: Crossway, 1991.

A Beka
Box 18000
Pensacola, FL 32523-9160
(800) 874-2352
Fax (800) 874-3592
e-mail: abbinfo@pcci.edu
http://www.pcci.edu/abb
Video classes available.

Alpha Omega Publications
P. O. Box 3153
Tempe, AZ 85281
(602) 731-9310

Alpha-phonics
The Elijah Company
Rt. 2, Box B, Fred Ford Rd

Crossville, TN 38555
(615) 456-6284
Fax (615) 456-6384

Alta Vista College Press Home
    School Curriculum
P.O. Box 222
Medina, WA 98039
(206) 454-7691

Amanda Bennett Unit Studies
P.O. Box 33293
Indiatlantic, FL 32903-0293

Associated Christian Schools
P.O. Box 27115
Indianapolis, IN 46227
(317) 881-7132

Association of Christian Schools
    International (ACSI)
P.O. Box 4097
Whittier, CA 90607-4097
(213) 694-4791
Character foundation curriculum.

Aves Science Kits
P.O. Box 229
Peru, ME 04290
(207) 562-7033
Specializes in home-school
    laboratory science.

Backyard Scientist
P.O. Box 16966
Irvine, CA 92713
Experiments children can do
    with household supplies.

Bob Jones University Press
Greenville, SC 29614
(800) 845-5731
Curriculum and standardized tests.

BrainQuest Cards
Workman Publishing
708 Broadway
New York, NY 10003-9555
Available at education supply
    stores, Wal-Mart, Sam's Club
    and libraries. Fun!

Bright Spark Press
20887 N. Springs Terrace
Boca Raton, FL 33428-1453
(407) 487-3199
Newsletter entitled *Bright Spark
    Super Learning Tools.*

Calvert School
105 Tuscany Rd.
Baltimore, MD 21210
(410) 243-6030
One teaching manual, everything
    needed for school year.

Cambridge Academy
1111 SW 17th St.
Ocala, FL 34474
(800) 252-3777
Fax (904) 620-0492
e-mail: CamAcad@aol.com

Carolina Biological Supply Company
2700 York Rd.
Burlington, NC 27215
(800) 334-5551
Supplies, live tadpoles, larvae and
    neat stuff; call for catalog.

Should I Home School?

Charlotte Mason Research and
Supply Co.
P.O. Box 172
Stanton, NJ 08885

Christian Book Distributors
P.O. Box 7000
Peabody, MA 01961-7000
(508) 977-5000
Christian books at great prices.

Christian Liberty Academy
Satellite Schools (CLASS)
502 W. Euclid Ave.
Arlington Heights, IL 60004
(847) 259-8736

Christian Life Workshops
Gregg Harris
P.O. Box 2250
Gresham, OR 97030
(503) 667-3942

Christian Light Publications
P.O. Box 1126
Harrisonburg, VA 22801-1126
(703) 434-0768

Classic Curriculum
Dept. G
P.O. Box 656
Milford, MI 48042
(313) 481-7008
Fax (800) 348-6688

Clonlara SchoolHome Based
Education Program
1289 Jewett
Ann Arbor, MI 48104
(313) 769-4511

*Constitutional Law for Christian
Students*
Constitutional Law Supplement
Both are available with Teacher
Handbook (teens through adults)
from Home School Legal Defense
Association.

Cornerstone Curriculum
2006 Flat Creek Place
Richardson, TX 75080
(214) 235-5149
David Quine's own materials plus
others.

Critical Thinking Press and Software
P.O. Box 448
Pacific Grove, CA 93950
(800) 458-4849
Fax (408) 372-3230

Cuisinaire Co. of America
P.O. Box 5026
White Plains, NY 10602-5026
(800) 237-3142
Fax (800) 551-RODS
Mathematical counting rods;
much more in their big catalog
also suitable for home schoolers.
Science stuff too.

Design-a-Study
408 Victoria Ave.
Wilmington, DE 19804
Create a custom curriculum!

Education Services
8825 Blue Mountain Dr.
Golden, CO 80403
(303) 234-5245

Fax (303) 231-0940

Educators Publishing Service
75 Moulton St.
Cambridge, MA 02138-1104
(800) 225-5750

ESP Inc.
1201 E. Johnson Ave.
P.O. Drawer 5080
Jonesboro, AR 72403-5080
(800) 643-0280

Family Learning Center (an
  imprint of Common Sense Press)
Rte. 2, Box 264
Hawthorne, FL 32643
(904) 475-5869

Great Christian Books
229 South Bridge St.
P.O. Box 8000
Elkton, MD 21922-8000
(800) 569-2481
Catalog of many materials you see
  here at discount prices!

Hands-On Equations
Borenson and Associates
P.O. Box 3328
Allentown, PA 18106
(215) 820-5575
Pre-algebra, grades 3-8.

Hewitt Research Foundation
P.O. Box 9
Washougal, WA 98671-0009
(206) 835-8708
Texts, other materials, personalized
book list. Christian-oriented; run

by Raymond and Dorothy Moore.

Home Education Press
P.O. Box 1083
Tonasket, WA 98855
(509) 486-1351

Home Study Alternative School
P.O. Box 10356
Newport Beach, CA 92658

Home Study Directory: National
  Home School Council
1601 18th St. NW
Washington, D.C. 20009

Home Study Institute
6940 Carroll Ave.
Takoma Park, MD 20912
(202) 723-0800

Home Study International
P.O. Box 4437
Silver Springs, MD 20914-4437

Hooked on Math and Hooked on
  Phonics
Gateway Educational Products
1045 W. Katella Ave., Ste. 200
Orange, CA 92662
(714) 633-2223
(800) ABC-DEFG

International Institute
P.O. Box 99
Park Ridge, IL 60068

International Linguistics
  Corporation
3505 E. Red Bridge Rd.

Kansas City, MO 64137
Foreign-language instruction tapes,
   books for young children;
   Chinese, English, French, German,
   Japanese, Russian, and more.

IQRA (Arabic for READ)
Attn: Dr. T. Ghazi
831 S. Laflin
Chicago, IL 60607
(312) 226-5694

John Holt's Book and Music Store
2269 Massachusetts Ave.
Cambridge, MA 02140
(617) 864-3100

Key Curriculum Press
P.O. Box 2304
Berkeley, CA 94702
(800) 338-7638
Innovative math workbooks.

Kolbe Academy
1600 F St.
Napa, CA 94559

KONOS Curriculum
P.O. Box 1534
Richardson, TX 75083
(214) 669-8337
Unit studies based on character
   qualities. You need separate
   language arts and math.

Latin Primer
Canon Press
P.O. Box 8741
Moscow, ID 83843
(800) 488-2034

Laurel Spring School, Ste. 201
P.O. Box 1440
Ojai, CA 93024
(800) 377-5890
(805) 646-0186

Lawrence Hall of Science
University of California
Berkeley, CA 94720
Science curriculum.

Learning at Home (Ann Ward)
P.O. Box 270-G
Honaunau, HI 96726

Living Heritage Academy
P.O. Box 1438
Lewisville, TX 75067

Math-U-See
Our Family Resources
1378 River Rd.
Drumore, PA 17518
(800) 383-9585
Curriculum and supplementary
   materials also.

McGuffey Academy
2213 Spur Trail
Grapevine, TX 76051
(817) 481-7008

Modern Curriculum Press
13900 Prospect Rd.
Cleveland, OH 44136
Textbooks, K-12, bilingual.

Moore Foundation
Box 1
Camas, WA 98607

National Book Co.
333 SW Park Ave.
Portland, OR 97205-3784
(503) 228-6345

Oak Meadow School
P.O. Box 712
Blacksburg, VA 24063
(703) 552-3263

Open Court
407 S. Dearborn
Chicago, IL 60605
Textbooks, K-12.

Our Family Resources
1378 River Rd.
Drumore, PA 17518
Curriculum and supplementary
materials.

Our Lady of the Rosary
105 E. Flaget Ave.
Bardstown, KY 40004
Catholic pre-K-12.

Our Lady of Victory School
4436 Alpine Dr.
P.O. Box 819
Post Falls, ID 83854

Pensacola Christian
  Correspondence School
Box 18000
Pensacola, FL 32523

Phoenix Special Programs
3132 W. Clarendon
Phoenix, AZ 85017

Potter's Press Preschool Curriculum
Shekinah Curriculum Cellar
967 Junipero Dr.
Costa Mesa, CA 92626

Rod & Staff Publishers
Hwy. 172
Crockett, KY 41413
(606) 522-4348
Solid Christian material

Saxon Publishing
1002 Lincoln Green
Norman, OK 73072
Basic math texts for independently
  working student.

Seton Home Study School
One Kidd Lane
Front Royal, VA 22630
(703) 636-9990
Catholic correspondence school.

Shekinah Curriculum Cellar
967 Junipero Drive
Costa Mesa, CA 92626
Books and teaching aids.

Sing, Spell, Read and Write
International Learning Systems
1000 112th Circle North, Ste. 100
St. Petersburg, FL 33716
(800) 321-8322

SMM Educational Services
P.O. Box 1079
Sunland, CA 91040
(818) 352-2310

Sonlight Curriculum
460 Snowy Owl Place
Highlands Ranch, CO 80126
(303) 470-1369
Christian, delight centered, with
    an international flavor.

Sycamore Tree
2179 Meyer Place
Costa Mesa, CA 92627
Per-family fee excludes
    registration/books; discounted
    materials. Includes testing,
    high-school transcripts and
    diploma. Must join Home
    School Legal Defense
    Association.

Teach Your Child to Read in 100
    Easy Lessons
Timberdoodle Company
E 1510 Spencer Lake Rd.
Shelton, WA 98584

Textbooks for Parents
P.O. Box 209
Kendrick, ID 83537

TOPS Learning Systems
10970 S. Mulino Rd.
Canby, OR 97013
Scientific activities and work-
    sheets on a variety of subjects.

Typical Course of Study
World Book Educational Products
101 Northwest Point Blvd.
Elk Grove Village, IL 60007
Scope and sequence for grades K-12.

Walch
321 Valley St., P.O. Box 658
Portland, ME 04014-0658
Textbooks 6-12.

Weekly Reader Skills Books
Field Publications
P.O. Box 16618
Columbus, OH 43285

World Eagle
64 Washburn Ave.
Wellesley, MA 02181
(800) 634-3805

The Writing Rd. to Reading
Reading Reform Foundation
P.O. Box 98785
Tacoma, WA 98498-0785
(206) 588-3436
Excellent and affordable spelling,
    reading and writing program.

Zephyr Press
P.O. Box 13448-B, Dept. 26
Tucson, AZ 85732-3448

In Canada
World Book Educational Products
    of Canada
Division of SFZ International
257 Finchdale Square Unit #2
Scarborough, Ontario M1X 1B9

High-School Curriculum
American School
2200 E. 170th St.
Lansing, IL 60438
(800) 228-5600

Cambridge Academy
1111 SW 17th St.
Ocala, FL 34474
(800) 252-3777
Fax (904) 620-0492
e-mail: CamAcad@aol.com

Keystone National High School
420 W. 5th St.
Bloomsburg, PA 17815
(800) 255-4937

North Dakota Division of Independent Study
State University Station
P.O. Box 5036
Fargo, ND 58105-5036
(701) 239-7282

Phoenix Special Programs
3132 W. Clarendon
Phoenix, AZ 85017

Sycamore Tree
2179 Meyer Place
Costa Mesa, CA 92627
Per-family fee does not include registration or books, but materials offered at a discount. Includes testing, high-school transcripts and diploma. Must join Home School Legal Defense Association. Catalog available to others.

Texas Technical University High School
Guided Study
P.O. Box 42191
Lubbock, TX 79409-2191

(800) MY COURS
(806) 742-2352, ext. 232

University of Nebraska-Lincoln
Independent Study High School
Division of Continuing Studies
269 Neb. Ctr. for Cont. Ed.
33rd and Holdredge Sts.
Lincoln, NE 68583-0900
(402) 472-4321

Educational Entertainment
TV Programs
Bill Nye the Science Guy
Kratt's Creatures
The Magic School Bus
Mr. Rogers' Neighborhood
Nova (various subjects)
National Geographic (various subjects)
Reading Rainbow
Sesame Street
Shining Time Station
Where in the World Is Carmen Sandiego?
Wishbone
You will have to watch these programs with your child to determine if they are age/interest/skill appropriate. (We were amazed to see our children enjoying programs that we would not have thought would interest them!)

Computer Software
The Magic Schoolbus (CD-ROM)
Explores the Ocean
Explores the Solar System
Explores the Human Body
Explores Inside the Earth

Scholastic/Microsoft Home Software
Ecoquest: The Search for Cetus (CD-ROM)
King's Quest series (CD-ROM or diskette)
Where in Time Is Carmen Sandiego?

Sierra On-Line
P.O. Box 3404
Salinas, CA 93912
(800) 757-7707

Magazines
Babybug (6 months to 2 years)
Ladybug (2-6 years)
Spider (6-9 years)
Cricket (9-14 years)
Cricket Magazine Group
P.O. Box 7434
Red Oak, IA 51591-2434
Excellent, literature-based magazines that feature puzzles, songs.

Kids Discover
P.O. Box 54206
Boulder, CO 80323-4206
Fascinating, superior-quality children's magazine (6-12 years). 10 issues per year: science, history, geography, arts, archaeology.

National Geographic World
National Geographic Society
P.O. Box 63171
Tampa, FL 33663-3177

Highlights for Children
P.O. Box 182167
Columbus, OH 43218-2167

Special Needs and Services
E-mail addresses are provided here for your convenience, but please note that they change often.

Books, Magazines, Videos
Assured Readiness for Learning
2452 Potter Rd., Ste. 364
Penn Yan, NY 14527
(315) 536-3034

At Our Own Pace
c/o Jean Kulczyk
102 Willow Dr.
Waukegan, IL 60087
Newsletter.

Barkley, Russell A. *ADHD: What Can We Do?* (video). New York: Guilford.
———. *ADHD: What Do We Know?* (video). New York: Guilford, 1992.

Closing the Gap/Communicating Together
P.O. Box 68
Henderson, MN 56044
(612) 248-3294
Bimonthly newsletter on computer use.

Escondido Tutorial Service
2634 Bernardo Ave.
Escondido, CA 92029
(619) 746-0980
e-mail: 74652.75@Compuserve.com

Exceptional Parent
P.O. Box 3000, Dept. EP
Denville, NJ 07834-9919
(800) 562-1973

Growing Without Schooling
2269 Massachusetts Ave.
Cambridge, MA 02140
(617) 864-3100

Hensley, Sharon C. *Home
Schooling Children with Special
Needs: Turning Challenges into
Opportunities.* Gresham, Ore:
Noble, 1995.

Herzog, Joyce. *Learning in Spite of
Disabilities.* Lebanon, Tenn.:
Greenleaf, 1994.
———. *Learning in Spite of Labels.*
Lebanon, Tenn.: Greenleaf, 1994.

Joyce Herzog
1440 San Juline Circle
St. Augustine, FL 32095
(800) 745-8212
Herzog presents workshops and
consults regarding curriculum
and special education.

Home Education Magazine
P.O. Box 1083
Tonasket, WA 98855
(509) 486-1351

The Home School Court Report
Home School Legal Defense
Association
P.O. Box 3000
Purcellville, VA 20134

(540) 338-5600
May be purchased apart from
membership.

Homemade Schooling
RR 1, Box 188
Atwood, IL 61913

Lane, Kenneth A. *Developing Your
Child for Success.* Lewisville,
Tex.: Learning Potentials, 1991.
Identifying learning difficulties
and developing therapy tech-
niques.

Parker, Harvey C. *ADAPT:
Attention Deficit Accommodation
Plan for Teaching.*
———. *The ADD Hyperactivity
Handbook for Schools.* Schools
Special Press, 1992.
———. *The ADD Hyperactivity
Workbook for Parents, Teachers
and Kids.* Schools Special Press,
1988.

The Special Needs Resource Guide
Great Books and Gifts
Peggy McKibben
9797 W. Colfax, #355
Lakewood, CO 80215

Sutton, Joe P. and Connie J.
*Strategies for Struggling Learners:
A Guide for the Teaching Parent.*
Simpsonville, S.C.: Exceptional
Diagnostics, 1995.
Available through
Exceptional Diagnostics
220 Douglas Dr.

Simpsonville, SC 29681
(803) 967-4729

Organizations and Services
These sources are for families who
find that their children do not fit
into the mainstream of education:
they are advanced for their age,
are having difficulty or are
known to have a specific handicap.

Academic Therapy Publications
20 Commercial Boulevard
Novato, CA 94949-6191
Directory of facilities and services
   for the learning disabled.

ADD Adult Mailing List
bl275@cleveland.freenet.edu

ADD Parents Support list
Dan Diaz
Majordomo@mv.mv.com

A.D.D. Warehouse (complete
catalog available upon request)
(800) 233-9273
(305) 792-8944
Fax (305) 792-8545
Many materials on learning and
   behavioral disabilities in
   children and adults.

ADHD/ADD 2000 Training
   Institutes
Medical Center of Central Georgia
Attn: Vivian Bozeman
4075 Elnora Dr., Suite 101
Macon, GA 31210
(800) 526-5952

Brochure on workshops held
   nationally for learning disabilities.

Adults with Attention Deficit
   Disorder
listserv@sjuvm.stjohns.edu

Almaden Valley Christian School
Sharon Hensley
6291 Vegas Dr.
San Jose, CA 95120
(408) 997-0290
Has an Internet services provider
   for home schoolers with special-
   needs children.

American Montessori Consulting
P.O. Box 5062
Rossmoor, CA 90720-5062
(310) 598-2321
e-mail: AMontessoriC@eworld.com

Apple of His Eye
Gerald and Donna Watanabe
95-1099 Lalai St.
Mililani, HI 96789

Association on Higher Education
   and Disability
P.O. Box 21192
Columbus, OH 43221-0192
(614) 488-4972

Autism Research Institute
182 Adams Ave.
San Diego, CA 92116

Avko Educational Research
   Foundation (for dyslexia)
3084 W. Willard Rd.

Clio, MI 48420
(810) 686-9283

Bipolar Depression/Disorder
Majordomo@ucar.edu

Bytes of Learning
(800) 465-6428
Software: Ultra Key and Ultra
  Writer (contains an auditory
  component).

CEC Membership
Council for Exceptional Children
1920 Association Dr., E30391
Reston, VA 22091-1589
(800) 8456-CEC
To order from CEC:
Publications Department, K50440
P.O. Box 79026
Baltimore, MD 21279-0026
Fax (703) 264-1637

CHADD
499 NW 70th Ave., Ste. 308
Plantation, FL 33317
(305) 587-3700

Christian Center for Educational
  Development
David and Kathryn Winters
Rt. 4, Box 300
Owatonna, MN 55060
(507) 451-8502
Consultation, workshops.

Creative Learning Resource Center
P.O. Box 829
North San Juan, CA 95959
(916) 292-3001

Diamonds
603 N. Third St.
Oskaloosa, IA 52577
Encouragement for caregivers of
  special-needs children.

Disabilities in Higher Education
DESSHE-L@ubvm.cc.Buffalo.edu

Disability Support of Families List
listserv@sjuvm.stjohns.edu

Disabled Children's Computer
  Group
P.O. Box 186
El Cerrito, CA 94530-0186

Exceptional Children's Assistance
  Center
P.O. Box 16
Davidson, NC 28036
(800) 962-6817
e-mail: cecpubs@cec.sped.ord

Free Spirit Publishing
400 1st Ave. N., Ste. 616
Minneapolis, MN 55401
(800) 735-7323
Fax (612) 337-5050
Publishes books for ADD, LD
  and gifted.

Georgiana Organization
P.O. Box 2607
Westport, CT 06880
(203) 454-1221
Information and curriculum for
  auditory training.

156

Hawthorne Educational Service
800 Gray Oak Dr.
Columbia, MO 65201
(314) 874-1710
(800) 542-1673
Fax (800) 442-9509

HEATH Resource Center
1 Dupont Circle NW, Ste. 800
Washington, DC 20036
(800) 544-3284
National clearinghouse for information about assistive technology.

Home School Legal Defense
  Association
P.O. Box 3000
Purcellville, VA 20134
(540) 338-5600

Homeschool ADDvisor
P.O. Box 118
Lincoln University, PA 19352

Homeschool Support Network
P.O. Box 140573
Gainesville, FL 32614-0573

Homeschooled Deaf Children
c/o the Agenbroads
116 Jerome
Silverton, OR 97381
(503) 873-8451

Information Technology and
  Disabilities Journal
listserv@sjuvm.stjohns.edu

Irlen Institute
5380 Village Rd.
Long Beach, CA 90808
(310) 429-8699
Helps assess and prescribe for
  scotopic sensitivity (visual
  learning disability).

Learning Development Network
Suzanne Stevens
134 Shady Blvd.
Winston-Salem NC 27101
(910) 723-8481
Supports families teaching disabled
  children at home.

Learning Disabilities Association
4156 Library Rd.
Pittsburgh, PA 15234

Learning Disabilities List
ld-list-request@curry.edu

LINCS-BBS
408-72707227
Settings: N81, to 14,400 Baud,
  3 lines
Free resource directory, shareware;
  needs, conditions and disabilities
  of children.

Love and Learning
Joe and Susan Kotlinski
P.O. Box 4088
Dearborn, MI 4812
(313) 581-8436

Multi-Handicapped Children
Didi Goodrich
2971 53rd SE

Auburn, WA 98002

MUMS (Mothers United for
    Moral Support)
150 Custer Court
Green Bay, WI 54301
(414) 336-5333
International parent-matching
    service (matches by condition).

NATHHAN
National Handicapped Home-
    schoolers Association Network
5383 Alpine Rd. SE
Olalla, WA 98359
(206) 857-4257
National Christian support group
    for families of special-needs
    home schoolers; newsletter.

NATHHAN Resource Guide by
    Kathy Salars
HC 31 51-N-91
Midland, TX 79707
Assists parents in selecting best
    materials for their special-needs
    child.

National Association for Down
    Syndrome
P.O. Box 4542
Oak Brook, IL 60522
(630) 325-9112

National Attention Deficit
    Disorder Association (ADDA)
P.O. Box 488
West Newbury, MA 01985
(800) 487-2282

National Council for Exceptional
    Children
(800) 328-0272
Special education information;
    will help you find a local group.

National Educational Association
    of Disabled Students (NEADS)
Carlton University
4th Level Unicentre
1125 Colonel By Drive
Ottawa, ON K1F 5B6
Canada
(613) 526-8008
Fax (613) 520-3704

National Handicapped Home-
    schooler's Association
814 Shaverton Rd.
Boothwyn, PA 19061
(215) 459-2035

National Home Education
    Research Institute
P.O. Box 13939
Salem, OR 97309
(503) 364-1490
Fax (503) 364-2827
Web: www.NHERI.ORG
e-mail: MAIL@NHERI.ORG

National Information Center for
    Children and Youth with
    Disabilities (NICHCY)
P.O. Box 1492
Washington, DC 20013
(800) 999-5599

National Organization for Rare
    Disorders

P.O. Box 8923
New Fairfield, CT 06812-8923
(203) 746-6518

National Parent Network on
  Disabilities (NPN)
1600 Prince St., Ste. 115
Alexandria, VA 22314
(703) 684-6763

National Reading Styles Institute
P.O. Box 737
Syosset, NY 11791
(800) 331-3117
Fax (516) 921-5500

Orton Dyslexia Society
Chester Building, Ste. 382
8600 LaSalle Rd.
Baltimore, MD 21286-2044
(410) 296-0232
(410) 321-5069

Parents of Gifted/LD Children
2420 Eccleston St.
Silver Spring, MD 20902
(301) 986-1422

Parents Instructing Challenged
  Children (PICC)
Allen and Barb Mulvey
615 Utica St.
Fulton, NY 13069
(315) 592-7257
Library and directory of families
  with special-needs children.

Parents' Newsletter on Special
  Education Law
P.O. Box 4571

Chapel Hill, NC 27515-4571

PRAISE (Parents Reaching
  Academically in Special
  Education)
Steven and Sheila Scott
570 Quincy
Grandville, MI 49418
(616) 896-6823

PREACCH (Parents Rearing and
  Educating Their Autistic
  Children in Christian Homes)
1960 E. Phillips Ct.
Merritt Island, FL 32952

Rebus Institute (works with LD
  population)
1400 Bayshore Blvd., Ste. 146
Burlingame, CA 94010
(415) 697-7424
Fax (415) 697-3734

Recorded Books (unabridged
  books on tape)
270 Skipjack Rd.
Prince Frederick, MD 20678
(800) 638-1304

Shepherd Boy
3211 W. Meadows Circle
Miramar, FL 33025
(305) 437-7784
Christian publication for
  families with autistic children.

SNAPS (Special Needs And
  Parent Support)
Joyce Harber
10411 Scott Mill Rd.

Jackonsville, FL 32257
(904) 268-3361

SJU Autism and Pervasive
  Developmental Disabilities List
listserv@sjuvm.stjohns.edu

SJU List for Coalition Advocating
  Disability Reform in Education
listserv@sjuvm.stjohns.edu

Special Children, Special
  Blessings
Jim and Debbie Mills
8266 Leucadia Ave.
San Diego, CA 92114
(619) 469-5822

Special Education Topics
Majordomo@virginia.edu

S.R.A. of McGraw-Hill
220 E. Danieldale Rd.
De Soto, TX 75115
(800) 843-8855

T.A.S.K. (Team of Advocates for
  Special Kids)
18685 Santa Ynez
Fountain Valley, CA 92708
(714) 962-6332

Technology Resources for People
  with Disabilities
2547 Eighth St.
Berkeley, CA 94710
(510) 841-DCCG

Treasures
Marcia Blackwood

6969 S. Meridian St.
Indianapolis, IN 46217
(317) 787-8611

Williams Syndrome
Waldene Addington
500 Trout
Troy, IL 62294
(618) 667-6402

Wilson Reading System
Barbara Wilson
162 W. Main St.
Millbury, MA 01527-1943

Woodbine House
(800) 843-7323
Publishes books on ADD, LD
  topics

World's Largest Selection of
  Unabridged Audio Books
(800) 626-3333

Support Groups and Associations
Alternative Approaches to
  Learning Discussion List
listserv@sjuvm.stjohns.edu

Alternative Education Resource
  Group—AERG
7 Bartlett St.
Moorabbin 3189
Victoria, Australia
Telephone: 9553 4720

Education Otherwise
36 Kinross Rd.
Leamington Spa
Warwickshire CV32 7EF

United Kingdom
Telephone: 0926 886828
Between ten and twenty thousand
  home-schooling families in
  Britain (great laws!).

Home School Legal Defense
  Association
P.O. Box 3000
Purcellville, VA 20134
(540) 338-5600
Free copy of "A Nationwide
  Study of Home Education."

Home Schooling List
Majordomo@world.std.com

Homeschool Associates of New
  England
116 Third Ave.
Auburn, ME 04210
(800) 882-2828
Fax (207) 777-0077

Jewish Home Educator's Network
1028 Albany St.
Schenectady, NY 12309

Kidsnet Mailing List
kidsnet-request@vms.cis.pitt.edu

Lake Arrowhead Education and
  Resource Network
P.O. Box 4901
Blue Jay, CA 92317
e-mail: rohare@aol.com

Moms In Touch International
P.O. Box 1120
Poway, CA 92074-1120

(800) 949-MOMS
Prayer groups for moms to
  support their local schools.

Restructuring Public Education
listserv@uhccvm.bitnet

Single Parents Educating Children
  in Alternative Learning
2 Pineview Dr., #5
Amelia, OH 45102

Taking Children Seriously
listserv@netcom.com

T.E.A.C.H. of Indiana
Steve Elder
308 E. Main St.
Fairland, IN 46126
(317) 835-0326

T.E.A.C.H. Institute (Minnesota)
Bob Newhouse
4350 Lakeland Ave. N.
Robbinsdale, MN 55422
(612) 535-5514

T.E.A.C.H. of New Jersey
Rob Stein
Ye Great St. & Bacon Neck Rd.
Greenwich, NJ 08323
(609) 451-8915

T.E.A.C.H. of North Carolina
Blake Talbot
7804 Hemlock Ct.
Raleigh, NC 27615
(919) 846-2556

UMOJA—UNIDAD—UNITED
A Newsletter for Homeschoolers
  of Color
c/o Kristin Cleage Williams
5621 S. Lakeshore Dr.
Idlewild, MI 49642

Y-Rights (Kid/Teen Rights
  Discussion Group)
listserv@sjuvm.stjohns.edu

**State Associations of Home
Educators**
Alabama
Christian Home Education
  Fellowship of Alabama
P.O. Box 563
Alabaster, AL 35007
(205) 664-2232

Alaska
Alaska Private and Home
  Educators Association
P.O. Box 141764
Anchorage, AK 99514
(907) 753-3018

Arizona
Arizona Families for Home
  Education
P.O. Box 4661
Scottsdale, AZ 85261-4661
(602) 443-0612

Christian Home Educators of
  Arizona
P.O. Box 13445
Scottsdale, AZ 85267-3445

Flagstaff Home Educators
6910 W. Suzette Lane
Flagstaff, AZ 86001-8220
(520) 774-0806

Arkansas
Arkansas Christian Home
  Education Association
P.O. Box 4410
North Little Rock, AR 72116
(501) 758-9099

California
Christian Home Educators
  Association
P.O. Box 2009
Norwalk, CA 90651
(800) 564-CHEA
Fax (310) 864-2432

Family Protection Ministries
910 Sunrise Ave., Ste. A-1
Roseville, CA 95661

Foothill Area Christian Home
  Educators
P.O. Box 958
Weimar, CA 95736
(916) 823-3164

Fremont Christian Home
  Educators
32311 Annette Court
Union City, CA 94587
(510) 796-4663

Sacramento Council of Parent
  Educators
P.O. Box 163178
Sacramento, CA 95816

(916) 444-4539

Valley Home Educators
  Association
1109 Rumble Rd.
Modesto, CA 95350
(209) 527-5471

Colorado
Christian Home Educators of
  Colorado
3739 E. 4th Ave.
Denver, CO 80206
(303) 388-1888

Concerned Parents for Colorado
P.O. Box 547
Florissant, CO 80902

Connecticut
Education Association of
  Christian Homeschoolers
25 Fieldstone Run
Farmington, CT 06032

Delaware
Delaware Home Education
  Association
P.O. Box 1003
Dover, DE 19903
(302) 368-3427

Tri-State Home School Network
P.O. Box 7193
Newark, DE 19714
(304) 368-4217

District of Columbia
Bolling Area Home Schoolers
  of D.C.

1516 E. Carswell Circle
Washington, DC 20336

Florida
Florida At Home
4644 Adanson
Orlando, FL 32804
(407) 740-8877

Florida Parent-Educators
  Association
P.O. Box 1372
Tallahassee, FL 32302-1372
(904) 224-7556

Georgia
Georgia Home Education
  Association
245 Buckeye Lane
Fayetteville, GA 30214
(404) 461-3657

North Georgia Home Education
  Association
200 W. Crest Rd.
Rossville, GA 30741

Georgia for Freedom in Education
209 Cobb St.
Palmetto, GA 30268
(404) 463-3719

Hawaii
Christian Homeschoolers of
  Hawaii
91-824 Oama St.
Ewa Beach, HI 96706
(808) 689-6398

Idaho
Idaho Home Educators
P.O. Box 4022
Boise, ID 83711
(208) 323-0230

Illinois
Illinois Christian Home
Educators
Box 261
Zion, IL 60099
(847) 670-7150

Christian Home Educators
Coalition
P.O. Box 470322
Chicago, IL 60647
(312) 279-0673

Indiana
Indiana Association of Home
Educators
850 N. Madison Ave.
Greenwood, IN 46142
(317) 859-1202

Iowa
Network of Iowa Christian Home
Educators
Box 158
Dexter, IA 50070
(515) 789-4310
Fax (800) 723-0438

Kansas
Christian Home Education
Confederation of Kansas
P.O. Box 3564
Shawnee Mission, KS 66203
(316) 945-0810

Kentucky
Christian Home Educators of
Kentucky
691 Howardstown Rd.
Hodgensville, KY 42748
(502) 358-9270

Kentucky Home Education
Association
P.O. Box 81
Winchester, KY 40392-0081
(606) 744-8562

Louisiana
Christian Home Educators
Association
P.O. Box 74292
Baton Rouge, LA 70874-4292
(504) 775-9709

Maine
Homeschoolers of Maine
P.O. Box 124
Hope, ME 04847
(207) 763-4251

Maryland
Christian Home Educators
Network
304 N. Beechwood Ave.
Catonsville, MD 21228
(410) 744-8919
Fax (410) 444-5465

Maryland Association of Christian
Home Education Organizations
P.O. Box 3964
Frederick, MD 21705
(301) 663-3999

164

Massachusetts
Mass. Home Schooling Organization of Parent Educators
15 Ohio St.
Wilmington, MA 01887
(508) 685-1061

Michigan
Information Network for Christian
Homes
4934 Cannonsburg Rd.
Belmont, MI 49306
(616) 874-5656

Minnesota
Minnesota Association of
Christian Home Educators
P.O. Box 32308
Fridley, MN 55432-0308
(612) 717-9070

Mississippi
Mississippi Home Educators
Association
109 Reagan Ranch Rd.
Laurel, MS 39440
(601) 649-8951

Missouri
Families for Home Education
400 E. High Point Lane
Columbia, MO 65203
(816) 826-9302

Missouri Association of Teaching
Christian Homes
307 E. Ash St., #146
Columbia, MO 65201
(573) 443-8217

Montana
Montana Coalition of Home
Educators
P.O. Box 654
Helena, MT 59624
(406) 587-6163

Nebraska
Nebraska Christian Home
Educators Association
P.O. Box 57041
Lincoln, NE 68505-7141
(402) 423-4297

Nevada
Home Education And Righteous
Training
P.O. Box 42262
Las Vegas, NV 89116
(702) 391-7219

Northern Nevada Home Schools
P.O. Box 21323
Reno, NV 89515
(702) 852-6647

New Hampshire
Christian Home Educators of
New Hampshire
P.O. Box 961
Manchester, NH 03105

New Jersey
Education Network of Christian
Homeschoolers
120 Mayfair Lane
Mount Laurel, NJ 08054
(609) 222-4283

New Mexico
Christian Association of Parent
  Educators of New Mexico
P.O. Box 2073
Farmington, NM 87002
(505) 898-3908

New York
Loving Education At Home
P.O. Box 88
Cato, NY 13033
(716) 346-0939

North Carolina
North Carolinians for Home
  Education
419 N. Boylan Ave.
Raleigh, NC 27603
(919) 834-6243

North Dakota
North Dakota Home School
  Association
4007 N. State St.
Rt. 5, Box 9
Bismarck, ND 58501
(701) 223-4080

Ohio
Christian Home Educators
  of Ohio
P.O. Box 262
Columbus, OH 43216
(614) 474-3177

Home Education Action
  Council of Ohio
P.O. Box 24133
Huber Heights, OH 45424
(513) 845-8428

Oklahoma
Christian Home Educators
  Fellowship of Oklahoma
P.O. Box 471363
Tulsa, OK 74147-1363
(918) 583-7323

Oklahoma Central Home
  Educators
P.O. Box 270601
Oklahoma City, OK 73137
(405) 521-8439

Oregon
Oregon Christian Home
  Education Association Network
2515 N.E. 37th
Portland, OR 97212
(503) 288-1285

Pennsylvania
Christian Home School
  Association of Pennsylvania
P.O. Box 3603
York, PA 17402-0603
(717) 661-2428

Pennsylvania Homeschoolers
R.D. 2, Box 117
Kittanning, PA 16201
(412) 783-6512

Rhode Island
Rhode Island Guild of Home
  Teachers
P.O. Box 11
Hope, RI 02831-0011
(401) 821-1546

South Carolina
South Carolina Association of
   Independent Home Schools
P.O. Box 2104
Irmo, SC 29063
(803) 551-1003

South Carolina Home Educators
   Association
P.O. Box 612
Lexington, SC 29071
(803) 951-8960

South Dakota
Western Dakota Christian
   Homeschools
P.O. Box 528
Black Hawk, SD 57118
(605) 660-2508

Tennessee
Tennessee Home Education
   Association
3677 Richbriar Ct.
Nashville, TN 37211
(615) 834-3529

Texas
Family Educators Alliance of
   South Texas
4719 Blanco Rd.
San Antonio, TX 78212
(210) 342-4674

Home-Oriented Private Education
   for Texas
P.O. Box 59876
Dallas, TX 75229-9876
(214) 358-2221

North Texas Home Education
   Network
P.O. Box 59627
Dallas, TX 75229
(214) 234-2366

South East Texas Home School
   Association
4950 F. M. 1960W, Ste. C3-87
Houston, TX 77069
(713) 370-8787

Texas Home School Coalition
P.O. Box 6982
Lubbock, TX 79493
(806) 797-4927

Utah
Utah Christian Homeschoolers
P.O. Box 3942
Salt Lake City, UT 84110-3942
(801) 296-7198

Vermont
Christian Home Educators of
   Vermont
2 Webster St.
Barre, VT 05641-4818
(802) 476-8821

Virginia
Home Educators Association of
   Virginia
P.O. Box 6745
Richmond, VA 23230-0745
(804) 288-1608

Washington
Washington Association of
   Teaching Christian Homes

N. 2904 Dora Rd.
Spokane, WA 99212

Washington Homeschool
Organization
18130 Midvale Ave. N.
Seattle, WA 98083

West Virginia
Christian Home Educators of
West Virginia
P.O. Box 8770
South Charleston, WV 25303
(304) 776-4664

Wisconsin
Wisconsin Christian Home
Educators
2307 Carmel Ave.
Racine, WI 53405
(414) 637-5127

Wyoming
Homeschoolers of Wyoming
221 West Spruce Street
Rawlins, WY 82301
(307) 324-5553

Associations in Canada
Alberta
Alberta Home Education
Association
Marvin Flynn, President
Box 1270
Lethbridge, AB T1J 4K1
(403) 320-0924
Fax (same)
e-mail: AHEA@TELUSPLANET.net

Home School Legal Defense
Association of Canada
#23295 3295 Dunmore Rd. SE
Medicine Hat, AB T1B 3R2
(403) 528-2704

British Columbia
Canadian Home Educators'
Association
SS 2, S-5, C-5
Kamloops, BC V2C 6C3

Canadian Home Educators
Association of British Columbia
c/o Vicki Livingstone
4684 Darin Court
Kelowna, BC V1W 2B3
(604) 764-7462

Greater Vancouver Home
Education Support Network
c/o Claudia Beaven & Philip
Toleikas
2636 Tennis Cres.
Vancouver, BC V6T 2E1
(604) 228-1939

Victoria Home Learning Network
c/o Cindy Barker
106-290 Regina Avenue
Victoria, BC V8Z 6S6

Manitoba
Manitoba Association for
Schooling at Home
89 Edkar Cres.
Winnipeg, MB R2G 3H8

New Brunswick
New Brunswick Association of
   Christian Homeschoolers
RR 1 Site 11 Box 1
Hillsborough, NB E0A 1X0

Northwest Territories
Gail and Ken Potter
Box 2285
Inuvik, NT X0E 0T0
(413) 979-3493

Rita Bernhardt
Box 1117
Fort Smith, NT X0E 0P0

Nova Scotia
Glen & Valerie Jordan
58 Flying Cloud Drive
Dartmouth, NS B2W 4S9

Nova Scotia Support Group
Laura Uhlman
RR 1
Pleasantville, NS B0R 1G0

Ontario
Canadian Alliance of
   Homeschoolers
RR 1
St. George, ON N0E 1N0
(519) 448-4001

Homeschoolers of Niagara
5929 Delaware St.
Niagara Falls, ON L2G 2E4

Ontario Federation of Teaching
   Parents
268 Butler St.

Woodstock, ON N4S 3B2

Orilla Homeschooler's Support
   Group
c/o Marge Black
45 Albert St. N.
Orilla, ON L3V 5K3

Rideau Valley Homeschooling
   Association
Box 313
N. Gower, ON K0A 2T0

T.E.A.C.H.
Ray Reyenga
333 King George Rd.
Brantford, ON N3R 5L9

Prince Edward Island
Peggy & Eddy Wargachuk
Box 120 RR 2
Richmond, PE C0B 1Y0

Quebec
Montreal Homeschoolers'
   Support Group
5241 Jacques Grenier
Montreal, PQ H3W 2G8
Sheryl Farrell: (514) 481-8435
Marie Bourque: (514) 484-0524

Quebec Homeschooling Advisory
4650 Acadia
Lachine, PQ H8T 1N5

Yukon
Yukon Home Educators Society
Debby La Roy
8 Normandy Road
Whitehorse, YT Y1A 3C5

Other Associations
England
Education Otherwise
36 Kinross Rd.
Leamington Spa,
Warks CV32 7EF
England
Telephone: 0926 886-828

Germany
Eifel Area Home Schoolers
52 SPTG/MW, UNIT 3640 Box 80
APO, AE 09126

Verna Lilly
PSC 118 Box 584
APO, AE 09137
011-49-6561-5341

Japan
KANTO Home Educators
  Association
PSC 477 Box 45
FPO, AP 96306-1299

New Zealand
Christian Home Schoolers of
  New Zealand
4 Tawa St.
Palmerston North, New Zealand

Puerto Rico
Christian Home Educators of the
  Caribbean
Palmas Del Mar Mail Service
Box 888, Ste. 273
Humacao, PR 00791
(809) 852-5284

Military
Christian Home Educators on
  Foreign Soil
Mike and Diane Smith
1856 CSGP, PSC2 Box 8462
APO, AE 09012

Radio
Home Education Radio Network
P.O. Box 3338
Idaho Springs, CO 80452
(303) 567-4092

Legal and Financial Information
Christian Financial Concepts
601 Broad St., SE
Gainsville, GA 30501

Home School Legal Defense
  Association
P.O. Box 3000
Purcellville, VA 20131
(540) 338-5600

Home School Legal Defense
  Association of Canada
#23295 3295 Dunmore Rd. SE
Medicine Hat, AB T1B 3R2
Canada
(403) 528-2704

Internet/On-line Services

The major on-line services (CompuServe, America Online, etc.) have forums and file areas devoted to (or of interest to) home schoolers. The Internet connects you to literally hundreds of sites maintained by or for home schoolers. Electronic addresses are not provided here, as any such list would be obsolete two hours after it was published. A good search program will point the way to sites or groups with the current "good stuff."

Try the following search words in your on-line service provider's main menu or your Web browser: home school; home schooling; alternate education.

Play Dough Recipe

2 c. water	2 tbsp. alum
$\frac{1}{2}$ c. salt	2 tbsp. cooking oil
food coloring	2 c. flour

Bring water, salt and food coloring to a boil in a 2-quart saucepan. Remove from heat. Add remaining ingredients and mix thoroughly. Empty mixture onto smooth, flat surface (countertop or large breadboard). Allow to cool slightly and knead while still warm. Store in an airtight container.